KÖNEMANN

© 2015 for this edition: koenemann.com GmbH
Distributed in cooperation with Frechmann Kolón GmbH

www.koenemann.com
www.frechmann.com

Published in the United States in 2016 by:

Skyhorse Publishing
307 West 36th Street, 11th Floor
New York, NY 10018, USA
T: +1 212 643 6816

info@skyhorsepublishing.com
www.skyhorsepublishing.com

Editorial project: LOFT Publications
Barcelona, Spain
Tel.: +34 932 688 088
Fax: +34 932 687 073
loft@loftpublications.com
www.loftpublications.com

Editorial coordinator: Simone K. Schleifer
Assistant to editorial coordination:
Aitana Lleonart Triquell
Editor: Loft Publications
Texts: Francesc Zamora Mola
Art director: Mireia Casanovas Soley
Design and layout coordination: Claudia Martínez Alonso
Layout: Cristina Simó Perales
Translations: Cillero & de Motta

ISBN 978-3-86407-310-6
ISBN 978-1-5107-0456-5 (Skyhorse, USA)

Printed in Spain

This inspiring book takes you on a visual journey to see the latest trends in contemporary international design of apartments throughout the world. It reveals innovative and eye-catching interior design ideas to make small apartments look attractive and feel inviting. Filled with beautiful photographs, this volume is also an essential resource for anyone looking to add comfort and usability to limited spaces.

Planning a small space requires confronting the challenge of finding creative solutions without sacrificing commodity and aesthetics. As you flip through the pages you will find examples of the remarkable possibilities in small space living.

There are two key elements in the design of reduced spaces. To furnish an apartment effectively, you have to think in terms of multi-functionality and flexibility. Many practical resources are available: for example, turn a dining area into a home office, or choose a coffee table that has storage space, such as a trunk. Custom-made furniture is a good option as it adapts well to the available space and conforms to the taste and needs of those who choose this option. Similarly, a single space can often be assigned various uses. Divide space to suit your needs with screens or bookshelves. A room divider can easily come handy in a studio apartment.

Storage is another issue we all fight with and creative solutions are much needed as it is easier for small apartments to become overrun with clutter. Beds with pull-out drawers, sofas that come with storage, room dividers with shelves, side tables, and ottomans can also provide storage space. In short, an infinite array of possibilities for taking the maximum advantage of the space available.

Once all these important aspects are under control, you can accessorize your apartment to make it more personal, inviting and comfortable. Through the numerous examples of visually attractive ideas, you will find solutions, some of which are easy to put into practice and, above all, very imaginative: wall papers, posters, paintings to dress up walls when you are not allowed to paint the walls; floor lamps, area rugs, curtains, etc. The multitude of examples shows designs that play with furniture arrangements, colors, textures, and light to meticulous detail.

The contemporary apartment is about making life more pleasant, comfortable and easy for the people living with space constraints that may represent the desire to simplify our lifestyle.

Ce livre, source d'inspiration, constitue un véritable voyage virtuel vers les dernières tendances internationales du design contemporain d'appartements. Il dévoile des idées innovantes et surprenantes de design intérieur visant à donner de l'allure et du cachet aux petits appartements. Regorgeant de superbes photos, ce volume est également une ressource indispensable pour toute personne cherchant à rendre des espaces limités plus confortables et pratiques.

Dans l'organisation de petits espaces, il est essentiel de relever le défi de trouver des solutions créatives sans pour autant sacrifier le confort ou l'esthétique. Au fil des pages, vous découvrirez des exemples surprenants des différentes possibilités qu'offrent les petits espaces de vie.

Le design des espaces réduits repose sur deux éléments clés. Afin de meubler correctement un appartement, il convient de penser en termes de multifonctionnalité et de flexibilité. Il existe de nombreuses solutions pratiques, comme par exemple transformer la salle à manger en bureau ou encore choisir une table d'appoint disposant d'espaces de rangement, telle qu'une malle. Les meubles personnalisés sont une bonne option car ils s'adaptent bien à la surface disponible tout en respectant les goûts et les besoins de chacun. De même, il est possible d'attribuer plusieurs fonctions à un seul et même espace, par exemple, en le divisant à l'aide de cloisons mobiles ou de bibliothèques afin qu'il s'adapte à vos besoins. Une cloison peut s'avérer très utile dans un studio.

Le rangement est un autre problème auquel nous devons tous faire face, ce pour quoi il est indispensable de trouver des solutions créatives car les petits appartements sont rapidement encombrés par le désordre. Des lits équipés de tiroirs, des canapés dotés de rangements, des étagères faisant office de cloisons, des dessertes ou encore des ottomanes peuvent apporter des espaces de rangement supplémentaires. En bref, il existe une infinité de possibilités permettant d'exploiter au maximum la surface disponible.

Une fois que ces aspects essentiels sont sous contrôle, vous pouvez ajouter des accessoires à votre appartement pour le rendre plus personnel, chaleureux et confortable. Vous pourrez trouver des solutions parmi les nombreuses propositions visuellement esthétiques présentées dans ce livre.

Certaines d'entre elles sont faciles à mettre en œuvre mais, surtout, très imaginatives : du papier peint, des posters, des tableaux pour habiller les murs que vous ne pouvez pas peindre, des lampes de sol, des tapis, des rideaux, etc. Cette multitude d'exemples est le reflet de designs jouant avec l'agencement du mobilier, les couleurs, les textures et la lumière jusque dans les moindres détails.

Le design contemporain aspire à rendre la vie plus plaisante, plus agréable et plus facile pour l es personnes confrontées à des espaces réduits, ce qui renvoie probablement à notre propre désir d'un mode de vie plus simple.

Dieser inspirierende Band nimmt Sie mit auf eine Reise zu den neuesten internationalen Trends im Bereich der zeitgenössischen Inneneinrichtung. Er stellt innovative Designideen vor, die kleine Wohnungen attraktiv und einladend wirken lassen. Die wunderschönen Fotos bieten hervorragende Anregungen für alle, die ihrem begrenzten Wohnraum mehr Komfort verleihen und den verfügbaren Raum optimal nutzen möchten.

Bei der Einrichtung einer kleinen Wohnung müssen kreative Lösungen gefunden werden, die jedoch weder den Komfort noch die Ästhetik einschränken sollten. Auf den folgenden Seiten finden Sie zahlreiche Beispiel für die erstaunlichen Möglichkeiten, die selbst ein kleines Zuhause bietet.

Um kleine Wohnungen klug einzurichten, sind zwei Schlüsselelemente zu beachten: Multifunktionalität und Flexibilität, die beispielsweise dadurch erreicht werden können, dass ein Essbereich in ein Home Office verwandelt wird oder man eine Truhe als Beistelltisch mit zusätzlichem Stauraum nutzt. Maßgefertigte Möbel nutzen den vorhandenen Platz hervorragend aus und entsprechen dem persönlichen Geschmack und den Bedürfnissen der Bewohner bis ins Detail. Außerdem kann ein einziger Raum mehrere Funktionen erfüllen, indem er mithilfe von Paravents oder Bücherregalen in verschiedene Bereiche unterteilt wird. Insbesondere in einer Einzimmerwohnung kann sich ein Raumteiler äußerst nützlich erweisen.

Stauraum kann man nie genug haben... daher sind insbesondere in kleinen Wohnungen, die schnell überladen und unordentlich wirken, kreative Lösungen gefragt: Betten mit integrierten Schubladen, Sofas mit extra Stauraum, Raumteiler mit Regalböden... auch Beistelltische, Ottomanen und Hocker können in ihrem Inneren Dinge verstauen. Kurzum, es gibt unzählige Möglichkeiten, um das Beste aus den herrschenden Platzverhältnissen herauszuholen.

Wurden alle diese Aspekte bei der Einrichtung berücksichtigt, kann die Wohnung anschließend mit Accessoires ausgestattet werden, um ihr eine persönliche Note zu verleihen und sie einladend und komfortabel zu gestalten. Unter den zahlreichen vorgestellten Wohnideen sind sicherlich auch für Sie einige passende Lösungen dabei, die einfach umzusetzen sind und von großer Kreativität zeugen. Wenn die Wandfarbe Ihrer Wohnung nicht verändert werden darf, greifen Sie bei der Raumgestaltung einfach auf Tapeten, Poster und Bilder zurück und nutzen Sie die Möglichkeiten, die Stehlampen, Teppiche, Vorhänge usw. bieten. Die vielfältigen Beispiele zeigen Interieurs, in denen auf ausgeklügelte Weise mit der Anordnung der Möbel sowie mit Farben, Texturen und Licht gespielt wird.

In den Wohnungen von heute geht es darum, das Leben auch bei beengten Platzverhältnissen angenehmer, komfortabler und leichter zu machen.

Dit inspirerende boek neemt u mee op een visuele reis langs de laatste trends op het gebied van hedendaags design van appartementen overal ter wereld. Het omvat innovatieve en opvallende ideeën voor interieurdesign om kleine flats te veranderen in gezellige en stijlvolle woningen. Dit boek vol met mooie foto's is eveneens een belangrijk hulpmiddel voor iedereen die kleine ruimten van comfort en utiliteit wil voorzien.

Voor de inrichting van een ruimte van geringe afmetingen moet de uitdaging worden aangegaan om creatieve oplossingen te zoeken zonder aan comfort en esthetiek in te boeten. Als u door dit boek bladert vindt u voorbeelden van frappante mogelijkheden om kleine woningen in te richten.

Er zijn twee sleutelelementen voor het ontwerp van kleine ruimten. Om een appartement op effectieve wijze in te richten moet men in termen van multifunctionaliteit en flexibiliteit denken. Er zijn veel praktische hulpmiddelen beschikbaar: zo kan een eethoek in thuiskantoor worden veranderd of kan gekozen worden voor een koffietafel met opbergruimte, zoals een hutkoffer. Op maat gemaakt meubilair is een goede optie aangezien het bij de beschikbare ruimte en de smaak en behoeften van degenen die voor deze optie kiezen past. Zo kan ook een enkele ruimte vaak voor diverse doeleinden worden gebruikt. Verdeel de ruimte naargelang uw behoeften met schermen of boekenkasten. Een kamerscherm kan heel handig zijn in een eenkamerflat.

Opbergruimte is een ander punt waarmee wij zullen worstelen. We zullen creatieve oplossingen nodig hebben, want kleine appartementen staan zomaar vol met rommel. Bedden met uitneembare laden, banken met opbergruimte onder de zittingen, kamerschermen met planken, bijzettafels en ottomanes kunnen eveneens bergruimte verschaffen. Kortom, er bestaat een keur van mogelijkheden om de beschikbare ruimte maximaal te benutten.

Zodra al deze belangrijke aspecten onder controle zijn, kunt u uw appartement voorzien van accessoires en hem persoonlijker, gezelliger en comfortabeler maken. Onder de talrijke voorbeelden van visueel aantrekkelijke ideeën zult u oplossingen vinden, waarvan sommige gemakkelijk in de praktijk kunnen worden gebracht, en die bovenal zeer fantasierijk zijn: behang, posters of schilderijen om de wanden te versieren wanneer u deze niet mag schilderen; het gebruik van o.a. staande lampen, vloerkleden en gordijnen. De vele voorbeelden laten ontwerpen zien die in alle detail met meubilairopstellingen, kleuren, texturen en licht spelen.

De in dit boek opgenomen voorstellen voor het interieurdesign van moderne appartementen hebben ten doel het leven aangenamer, gerieflijker en gemakkelijker te maken voor mensen die te kampen hebben met ruimtegebrek en hun levensstijl willen vereenvoudigen.

Questo libro ricco di ispirazioni guiderà il lettore alla scoperta delle ultime tendenze nella progettazione contemporanea degli appartamenti in varie parti del mondo. Propone idee innovative e accattivanti sul design d'interni per trasformare piccole abitazioni in spazi accoglienti e ricchi di stile. Arricchito da magnifiche foto, questo volume rappresenta una risorsa essenziale per chiunque desideri aggiungere un tocco di comfort e praticità a uno spazio ridotto.

La pianificazione di uno spazio di piccole dimensioni richiede soluzioni inventive senza rinunciare alla comodità o all'estetica. In queste pagine sono riportati vari esempi sulle incredibili possibilità per organizzare al meglio i piccoli appartamenti.

La progettazione di spazi ridotti parte da due elementi chiave. Per arredare un appartamento in modo efficace occorre pensare in termini di multifunzionalità e flessibilità. Le soluzioni disponibili sono molteplici, come ad esempio trasformare un tinello in studio o scegliere un tavolino da caffè con spazio di contenimento come un baule. Gli arredi personalizzati sono una soluzione ottimale in quanto si adattano allo spazio disponibile, ai gusti e alle necessità di ciascuno. Analogamente, uno stesso spazio può spesso svolgere più funzioni. È importante suddividere lo spazio in base alle proprie necessità attraverso l'uso di pareti mobili o librerie. Un paravento può essere una soluzione pratica in un monolocale.

Lo spazio di contenimento è un altro aspetto con cui fare i conti; offrire soluzioni creative è imprescindibile dato che un appartamento di piccole dimensioni tende a saturarsi con facilità e molto rapidamente. Letti dotati di cassetti estraibili, divani con spazio di contenimento sotto le sedute, pareti divisorie dotate di ripiani, angoliere e puff possono servire da contenitori. Insomma, infinite possibilità per sfruttare al massimo lo spazio disponibile.

Una volta risolti tutti questi aspetti essenziali, è possibile utilizzare gli elementi decorativi per dare al proprio appartamento un tocco più personale, accogliente e confortevole. Nei numerosi esempi di idee visivamente accattivanti il lettore troverà molte soluzioni, alcune delle quali facili da realizzare e, soprattutto, molto creative: uso di carta da parati, poster o quadri per decorare le pareti quando non è possibile dipingerle; uso di lampade con piantana, tappeti o tende per delimitare le varie zone, ecc. I molteplici esempi mostrano progetti che giocano con la disposizione degli arredi, con colori, finiture e luci dai dettagli meticolosi.

Queste proposte di arredo per gli appartamenti contemporanei hanno come scopo rendere la vita più piacevole, comoda e facile a coloro che convivono con limiti di spazio e desiderano semplificare il proprio stile di vita.

Este inspirador libro conducirá al lector de viaje por las últimas tendencias del diseño contemporáneo de apartamentos en todo el mundo. Incorpora ideas de interiorismo innovadoras y vistosas para transformar viviendas pequeñas en espacios acogedores y con estilo. Repleto de magníficas fotografías, este volumen constituye asimismo un recurso esencial para cualquiera que desee aportar un toque de comodidad y practicidad a un espacio reducido.

La planificación de un espacio de pequeñas dimensiones exige afrontar el desafío de hallar soluciones inventivas sin sacrificar la comodidad ni la estética. En estas páginas encontrará ejemplos de las asombrosas posibilidades existentes para organizar viviendas pequeñas.

El diseño de espacios reducidos parte de dos elementos clave. Para amueblar un apartamento de manera eficaz hay que pensar en términos de multifuncionalidad y flexibilidad. Existen muchos recursos prácticos disponibles: transformar un comedor en un despacho o seleccionar una mesa de café con espacio de almacenaje, como, por ejemplo, un baúl. El mobiliario personalizado es una opción fantástica, pues se adapta al espacio disponible y a los gustos y las necesidades de cada cual. En la misma línea, un mismo espacio puede a menudo cumplir varios usos. Puede dividirse el espacio en función de las necesidades mediante biombos o librerías: una mampara separadora puede resultar práctica en un estudio de un solo ambiente.

El espacio de almacenaje es otro aspecto con el que hay que lidiar, y dar con soluciones creativas es imprescindible, pues es fácil que un apartamento pequeño quede abarrotado de trastos rápidamente. Camas con cajones extraíbles, sofás con espacio de almacenaje bajo los asientos, mamparas divisoras con estanterías, mesillas rinconeras y otomanas pueden hacer las veces de pequeños armarios. En suma, hay un sinfín de posibilidades para sacar el máximo provecho al espacio disponible.

Una vez que todos estos aspectos esenciales están bajo control, se puede usar la decoración para imprimir al apartamento un aire más personal, acogedor y confortable. En las ideas visualmente atractivas que se presentan a continuación se recogen multitud de soluciones, algunas de las cuales resultan fáciles de poner en práctica y que son, sobre todo, muy imaginativas: uso de papeles pintados, pósters o pinturas para decorar paredes cuando el inquilino tiene prohibido pintarlas; empleo de lámparas de pie, alfombras o cortinas para delimitar zonas... Los múltiples ejemplos muestran diseños que juegan con disposiciones de mobiliario, colores, texturas y luces con un grado de detalle meticuloso.

Estas propuestas de decoración de apartamentos contemporáneos tienen el fin de hacer la vida más agradable, cómoda y fácil a aquellas personas que viven con limitaciones de espacio y pueden representar el deseo de simplificar nuestro estilo de vida.

STUDIOS

STUDIOS

EINZIMMERWOHNUNGEN

EENKAMERFLATS

MONOLOCALE

ESTUDIOS DE UN SOLO AMBIENTE

The biggest downsize when living in a studio apartment is usually the lack of storage space. How do we fit so much in so little space? And how could we possibly manage to make the space look great and not make it look cluttered?

The goal of decorating a studio apartment should be to convert it into a living space that is appealing, functional and comfortable. The best approach to achieve this goal should begin by designating specific areas for sleeping, eating, working and any activity that is part of your daily lifestyle.

Utility has to be the first priority. It is critical that you furnish your little space with adequate functional pieces of furniture. You'll find that furniture that fulfills multiple functions is best suited for a space of limited proportions.

Studio apartments also arise the difficulty of creating a private zone, that of sleeping for example. This situation offers the opportunity for creative solutions to divide a room without segmenting the space excessively. There are endless options to use fabrics and curtains to your advantage. Sheer fabrics, bead curtains and any other hanging objects that come into your imagination can be a perfect room divider when you need to screen off a section of your studio. They are also mobile, which means that they offer the flexibility to change the configuration of the studio as needed and manage one-room living as comfortably as possible.

Le plus grand inconvénient d'un studio est généralement le manque d'espaces de rangement. Comment garder autant de choses dans un si petit espace et comment le transformer en une superbe pièce sans qu'elle ne semble trop encombrée ?

L'objectif de la décoration d'un studio doit être d'en faire un espace de vie esthétique, fonctionnel et confortable. La meilleure approche pour atteindre ce but est de commencer par délimiter les zones utilisées pour dormir, manger, travailler ou réaliser toute autre activité faisant partie intégrante de votre vie quotidienne.

La commodité doit être la priorité. Il est essentiel de meubler votre petit espace avec des meubles adéquats et fonctionnels. Rien de mieux que des meubles remplissant différentes fonctions pour agencer un espace aux dimensions restreintes. Dans un studio, une autre difficulté est de créer un espace privé, comme le coin nuit. Cette situation permet d'opter pour des solutions créatives afin de diviser la pièce sans trop segmenter l'espace. Il existe une multitude de possibilités pour utiliser les tissus et les rideaux à votre avantage. Les tissus légers, les rideaux en perles et toute sorte d'objets suspendus qui vous viennent à l'esprit peuvent constituer une cloison idéale si vous souhaitez dissimuler une partie de votre studio. Ils sont également mobiles, ce qui permet de changer la configuration de l'appartement au besoin et de vivre dans une seule pièce le plus confortablement possible.

Der größte Nachteil einer Einzimmerwohnung besteht für gewöhnlich im Mangel an Stauraum. Wie soll eine ganze Einrichtung auf so kleiner Fläche Platz finden? Und wie erreicht man, dass das Appartement toll aussieht und nicht überladen und vollgestopft wirkt?

Beim Einrichten einer Einzimmerwohnung sollte darauf abgezielt werden, einen Wohnraum zu gestalten, der einladend, funktionell und komfortabel ist. Dies erreicht man am besten, indem man zunächst verschiedene Bereiche zum Schlafen, Essen, Arbeiten und für die sonstigen Tätigkeiten des alltäglichen Lebens einteilt.

Die wichtigste Rolle spielt hierbei stets der praktische Nutzen. Hierbei ist besonders darauf zu achten, dass der beengte Wohnraum mit entsprechenden, möglichst zweckmäßigen Möbelstücken ausgestattet wird. Sie werden feststellen, dass Vielzweckmöbel bei beschränkten Platzverhältnissen am besten geeignet sind.

Eine weitere Schwierigkeit bei der Einrichtung von Einzimmerwohnungen besteht darin, ausreichend Privatsphäre (z. B. im Schlafbereich) zu schaffen. Hier sind kreative Lösungen gefragt, um den Raum in verschiedene Zonen einzuteilen, ohne ihn noch kleiner wirken zu lassen... Dies gelingt beispielsweise mithilfe von dünnen Stoffen, Perlenvorhängen und anderen hängenden Objekten, die sich als ideale Raumteiler erweisen, wenn es darum geht, einen bestimmten Bereich vom Rest der Einzimmerwohnung abzutrennen. Derartige Raumteiler sind außerdem mobil einsetzbar und bieten daher die gewünschte Flexibilität, um die Raumaufteilung nach Bedarf zu ändern und ein möglichst komfortables Wohnen in einem Einzimmerappartement zu ermöglichen.

Het grootste ongemak om in een eenkamerflat te wonen is het gebrek aan bergruimte. Hoe kunnen zoveel mogelijk spullen in zo weinig ruimte worden ondergebracht? En hoe kan de ruimte met stijl worden ingericht zonder propvol te lijken?

De bedoeling van de inrichting van een studio is deze te veranderen in een mooie, functionele en comfortabele woonruimte. De beste manier om dit doel te bereiken is het ontwerpen van specifieke zones om te slapen, te eten, te werken en voor elke andere activiteit die deel uitmaakt van het dagelijkse leven.

Nuttigheid moet voorrang krijgen. Het is belangrijk dat u uw kleine ruimte met geschikt en functioneel meubilair inricht. Er zijn meubels te vinden die aan vele functies voldoen en de beste optie zijn voor een ruimte van geringe afmetingen. Eenkamerappartementen vormen ook een probleem bij het creëren van een privézone, bijvoorbeeld om te slapen. Deze situatie stelt u in de gelegenheid om creatieve oplossingen te zoeken en een vertrek in te delen zonder de ruimte te veel te segmenteren. Er zijn oneindig veel mogelijkheden om stoffen en gordijnen te gebruiken. Doorzichtige stoffen, kralengordijnen en andere hangende voorwerpen die tot uw verbeelding spreken zijn perfecte kamerschermen wanneer u een deel van uw studio moet afschermen. Bovendien zijn ze beweegbaar en dus flexibel, waardoor u gemakkelijk de indeling van het appartement kunt wijzigen en de eenkamerruimte met zoveel mogelijk comfort kunt inrichten.

Il principale inconveniente di vivere in un appartamento composto da un unico ambiente è la mancanza di spazio di contenimento. Come sistemare tante cose in così poco spazio? E come fare in modo che lo spazio abbia stile senza saturarsi e risultare caotico?

Arredare un monolocale significa trasformarlo in uno spazio abitabile carino, funzionale e confortevole. Per ottenere questo risultato, la migliore cosa da fare è definire le zone specifiche in cui dormire, mangiare, lavorare e svolgere qualsiasi altra attività quotidiana.

L'utilità rappresenta la priorità assoluta. È essenziale arredare questo piccolo spazio con elementi adeguati e funzionali. Sul mercato sono presenti mobili versatili, la migliore opzione per spazi di dimensioni ridotte.

I monolocali presentano anche la difficoltà di creare una zona privata, ad esempio per dormire. Per trasformare questo problema in un'opportunità, basta applicare soluzioni creative per dividere un ambiente senza segmentare eccessivamente lo spazio. Vi sono infinite opzioni che vedono l'impiego di tessuti e tende a questo scopo. I tessuti trasparenti, le tende di perline e oggetti sospesi di qualsiasi altro tipo possono servire da elementi di separazione tra gli ambienti quando si rende necessario isolare una zona del monolocale. Inoltre, trattandosi di oggetti mobili, offrono la flessibilità di modificare la configurazione dell'appartamento e gestire lo spazio unico con la massima comodità possibile.

El mayor inconveniente de vivir en un apartamento de un solo ambiente es la falta de espacio de almacenaje. ¿Cómo meter tantas cosas en tan poco sitio? ¿Y cómo conseguir que el espacio tenga estilo sin parecer abarrotado?

El objetivo de decorar un estudio debería ser convertirlo en un espacio habitable bonito, funcional y confortable. El mejor planteamiento para tal fin pasa por designar zonas específicas para dormir, comer, trabajar y desarrollar cualquier otra actividad que forme parte de la vida cotidiana.

La utilidad es la principal prioridad. Es esencial que amueble su pequeño espacio con mobiliario adecuado y funcional. El mercado ofrece una gran variedad de muebles versátiles, la mejor opción para un espacio de dimensiones reducidas.

Los apartamentos de un solo ambiente también plantean la dificultad de crear una zona privada, por ejemplo, para dormir. Ese desafío puede convertirse en oportunidad aplicando soluciones creativas para dividir una estancia sin segmentar el espacio en exceso. Existen opciones infinitas de tejidos y cortinas con este fin. Las telas transparentes, las cortinas de cuentas y otros objetos colgantes que acudan a nuestra imaginación pueden servir como separadores de ambientes cuando necesitamos apantallar una zona del estudio. Además, son móviles, lo cual implica que brindan la flexibilidad de modificar la configuración del apartamento y gestionar el espacio único con la máxima comodidad posible.

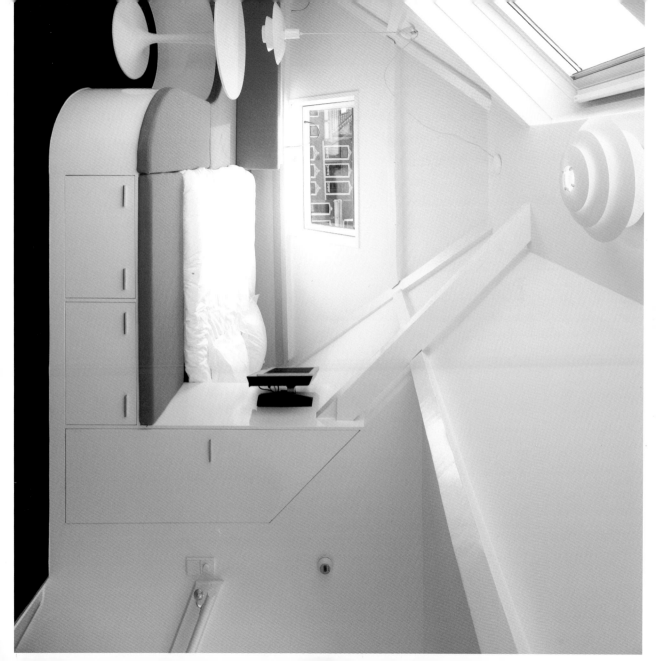

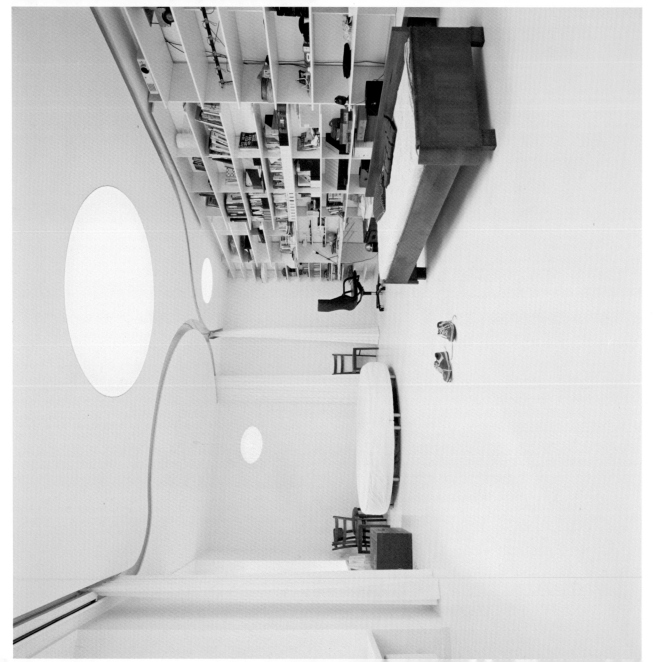

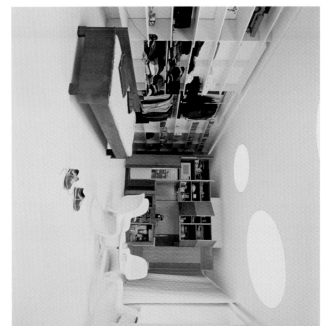

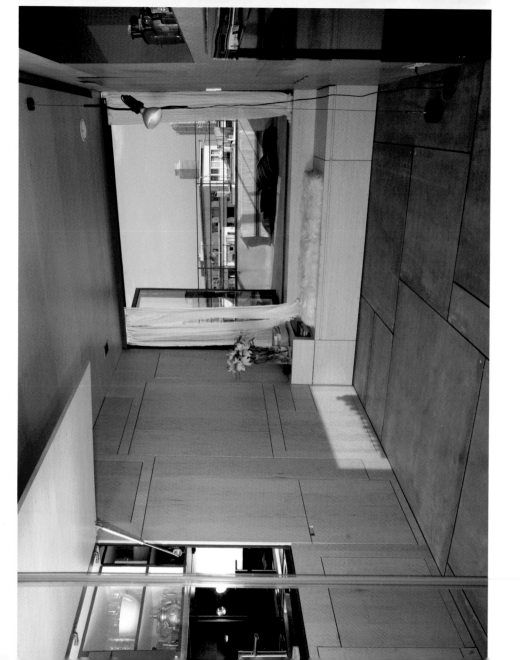

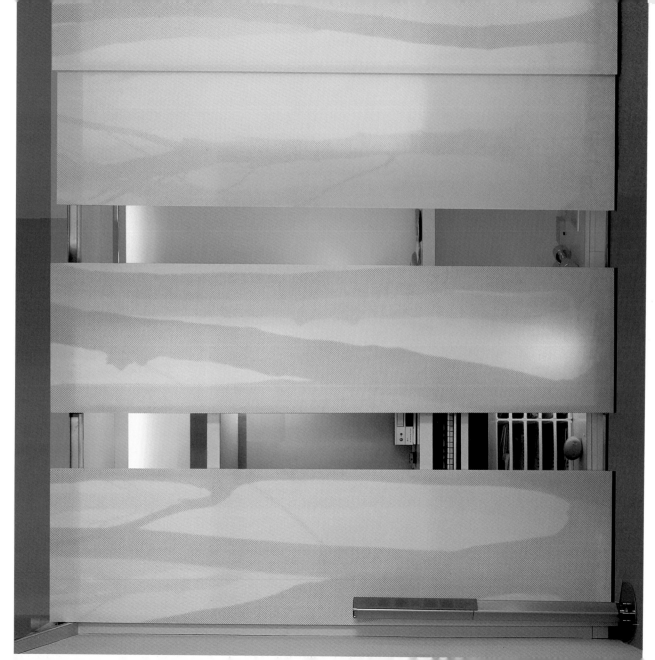

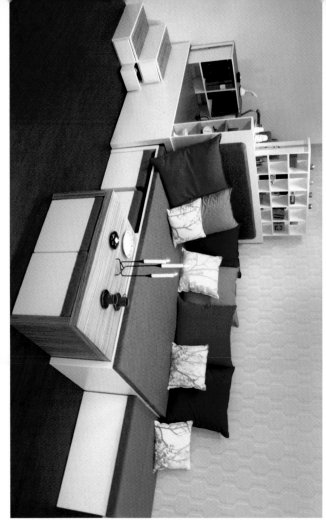

HALL VESTIBULES

VESTIBULES D'ENTRÉE

EINGANGSBEREICH

HALLEN

DISIMPEGNO

RECIBIDORES

The vestibule is an introduction to what your guests will find in the rest of the apartment. It is also the space most suitable to store coats, jackets, shoes, hats, umbrellas, etc. So while you want it to make a good impression, you also need it to be functional. There are plenty of furniture and accessories to choose from designed to fulfill this storage function. In case you have an entry door that leads directly to the living area, consider creating a small vestibule by placing a room divider that will provide you with some privacy and will mark a sense of entry. This should not get in the way of natural light reaching the vestibule. Fabric or bead curtains work well without segmenting the apartment.

Even though the hallway is generally a space you just walk through, it should be included in you decorating plans as any other room in the apartment. Usually adding a touch of color to your hallway is enough to spice it up. Hall rugs are also a good solution. But what really will determine your decorating decisions is the proportions of your hallway. If it is wide enough, you can place some narrow pieces of furniture as accent items such as a long, narrow table or chest of drawers with a couple of chair on each side. If this option is not viable, hang framed pictures or small artwork on the walls: the visual impact is quite efficient. Do not cover the entire length of the wall though. A few well-chosen pieces will create a good effect and will not crowd the already long and narrow passage.

Le vestibule est une introduction à votre appartement. Il s'agit également de l'espace le mieux adapté pour ranger manteaux, vestes, chaussures, chapeaux, parapluies, etc. Ainsi, cet espace doit être à la fois esthétique et fonctionnel. Il existe tout un tas de meubles et d'accessoires à choisir pour remplir cette fonction de stockage. Si vous avez une porte d'entrée conduisant directement à l'espace de vie, vous pouvez créer un petit vestibule en plaçant une cloison qui vous procurera une certaine intimité et délimitera une sorte d'entrée. Toutefois, cela ne doit pas entraver le passage de la lumière naturelle dans le vestibule. Des rideaux en tissu ou en perles sont une bonne option qui ne segmente pas l'appartement.

Même si l'entrée est généralement un espace où l'on ne fait que passer, elle doit s'intégrer aux plans de décoration, tout comme les autres pièces de l'appartement. En général, une petite touche de couleur suffit pour rehausser le vestibule. Les tapis sont également une bonne solution. Cependant, ce sont les dimensions de votre entrée qui détermineront réellement vos choix de décoration. Si elle est assez large, vous pourrez y placer quelques meubles étroits comme par exemple une longue table étroite ou encore une commode avec des chaises de chaque côté. Si cette option n'est pas possible, accrochez simplement des photos encadrées ou de petits tableaux sur les murs : effet garanti. Veillez cependant à ne pas couvrir le mur en entier. Quelques meubles bien choisis peuvent créer un bel effet sans encombrer un passage déjà long et étroit.

Der Eingangsbereich vermittelt Ihren Gästen einen ersten Eindruck von Ihrer Wohnung und bietet sich außerdem für die Aufbewahrung von Mänteln, Jacken, Schuhen, Kopfbedeckungen, Schirmen usw. an. Daher sollte dieser Bereich sowohl einladend und aufgeräumt wirken und gleichzeitig funktionell gestaltet sein. Die große Auswahl an erhältlichen Möbelstücken und Wohnaccessoires erleichtert eine Einrichtung, die Stauraum bietet. Falls Ihre Eingangstür direkt ins Wohnzimmer führt, kann mithilfe eines Raumteilers ein kleiner Vorraum geschaffen werden, der den Eingangsbereich begrenzt und für mehr Privatsphäre sorgt. Dabei sollte darauf geachtet werden, dass ausreichend Tageslicht in die neu geschaffene Diele fällt. Stoff- oder Perlenvorhänge leisten in diesem Sinne gute Dienste und sorgen für eine lockere, nicht zu scharfe Abtrennung.

Auch wenn der Flur im Allgemeinen ein Durchgangsbereich ist, sollte er genau wie jeder andere Raum in der Wohnung in die Gestaltung einbezogen werden. Meist genügt bereits ein kleiner Farbtupfer oder ein schöner Läufer, um den Eingangsbereich aufzupeppen. Der wichtigste Aspekt, der die Einrichtung des Flurs wesentlich beeinflusst, sind dessen Proportionen. Ist der Gang breit genug, können mit einigen schmalen Möbelstücken Akzente gesetzt werden – beispielsweise mit einem langen Sideboard oder einem Schubladenschrank, neben dem ein paar Stühle platziert werden. Ist diese Option nicht durchführbar, kann man bereits durch das Aufhängen einiger gerahmten Bilder oder kleiner Kunstwerke eine bedeutende optische Wirkung erzielen. Hierbei ist jedoch darauf zu achten, die Wand nicht auf ihrer ganzen Länge zu dekorieren. Einige wenige sorgfältig ausgewählte Stücke sorgen für eine angenehme Wirkung und lassen einen langen, engen Flur nicht überladen aussehen.

De hal is de introductie van wat uw gasten in de rest van uw woning zullen vinden. Het is ook de meest geschikte ruimte om onder andere jassen, schoenen, hoeden en paraplu's te bewaren. Hoewel men een goede indruk met de entree wil maken, is het met name van belang dat hij functioneel is. U kunt uit een keur van meubels en accessoires kiezen om aan deze opbergfunctie te voldoen. Als uw voordeur direct uitkomt op de woonkamer, kunt u overwegen om een kleine hal te creëren door een tussenschot te plaatsen dat een zekere privacy verschaft en het gevoel geeft dat u een kamer binnenloopt. Dit scherm mag de inval van natuurlijk licht in de hal niet verhinderen. Stoffen of kralengordijnen voldoen aan dit doel zonder de woning in segmenten op te delen.

Ondanks het feit dat de hal gewoonlijk een ruimte is die alleen als verbindingsruimte fungeert, dient hij net als elk ander vertrek van uw woning in uw decoratieplannen te worden opgenomen. Gewoonlijk is het voldoende om de hal wat kleur te geven opdat hij persoonlijkheid krijgt. Vloerkleden zijn ook een goede oplossing. Wat de beslissing over het ontwerp werkelijk bepaalt zijn de verhoudingen van de ruimte. Als de hal breed genoeg is, kunt u er een smal meubel, zoals een tafel of lange, smalle ladenkast neerzetten met aan weerszijden een paar stoelen. Als deze optie niet haalbaar is, dan zorgen foto's of ingelijste schilderijen aan de wanden voor voldoende visueel effect. Maar hang de wand niet te vol met foto's. Een aantal goed uitgekozen afbeeldingen brengt een beter effect teweeg en overlaadt dit gewoonlijk lange en smalle vertrek niet.

Il disimpegno o l'ingresso è uno spazio che introduce gli ospiti al resto della casa. È anche il luogo ideale in cui riporre cappotti, giacche, scarpe, cappelli, ombrelli, ecc. Si tratta quindi di uno spazio che deve offrire un elevato valore estetico senza però rinunciare alla funzionalità. Vi sono moltissimi mobili e accessori tra cui scegliere per svolgere questa funzione di contenimento. Qualora la porta di ingresso si apra direttamente sul salotto, potrebbe essere utile realizzare un piccolo ambiente inserendo un divisorio, in modo da offrire una certa privacy e trasmettere la sensazione di entrare in una stanza. Il divisorio non deve ostacolare l'entrata di luce naturale nell'ingresso. Le tende di tessuto o perline svolgono questo ruolo senza segmentare la casa.

Nonostante l'ingresso sia solitamente uno spazio che svolge una mera funzione di comunicazione, deve essere considerato e arredato come qualsiasi altro ambiente della casa. Normalmente basta un tocco di colore per trasmettere personalità. Anche i tappeti sono una buona soluzione. Tuttavia, l'elemento davvero determinante saranno le sue proporzioni. Se è sufficientemente ampio, sarà possibile sistemarvi un mobile stretto come un tavolino o una cassettiera lunga e stretta con un paio di sedie ai lati. Se questa opzione non è percorribile, si potranno appendere alle pareti delle foto o dei quadri incorniciati per creare un sufficiente impatto visivo. Evitare però di riempire eccessivamente la parte di immagini. Pochi pezzi scelti accuratamente trasmettono un effetto migliore e non sovraccaricano l'ambiente, che per sua natura è lungo e stretto.

El recibidor es una introducción a lo que sus invitados hallarán en el resto de la vivienda. Es también el espacio más adecuado para guardar abrigos, chaquetas, zapatos, sombreros, paraguas, etc. De manera que, aunque por un lado se desee dar buena impresión con él, es fundamental que sea funcional. Hay multitud de muebles y accesorios entre los que elegir para cumplir esta función de almacenaje. En caso de contar con una puerta de entrada que abra directamente al salón, plantéese crear un pequeño vestíbulo instalando un separador de ambientes que le proporcione cierta privacidad y transmita la sensación de entrar a una estancia. Esta mampara no debe obstaculizar la entrada de luz natural al vestíbulo. Las cortinas de tela o de cuentas cumplen este objetivo sin segmentar la vivienda.

Pese a que el vestíbulo suele ser un espacio que solo cumple una función comunicadora, debería incluirse en los planes de decoración tal como cualquier otra estancia del apartamento. Las alfombras también son una buena solución. Sin embargo, lo que realmente determinará las decisiones de diseño serán las proporciones que presente. Si es lo bastante amplio, puede colocarse un mueble estrecho, como una mesa o una cajonera larga y estrecha con un par de sillas a cada lado. Si esta opción no es viable, colgar de las paredes unas fotografías o unos cuadros enmarcados causa un impacto visual suficiente. Con todo, no conviene abarrotar la pared de imágenes. Unas cuantas piezas bien escogidas transmiten mejor efecto y no recargan esta estancia por naturaleza larga y estrecha.

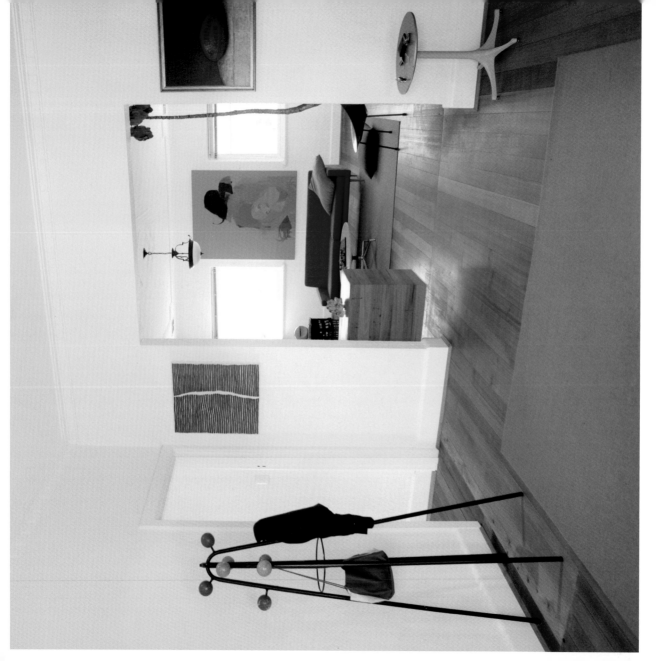

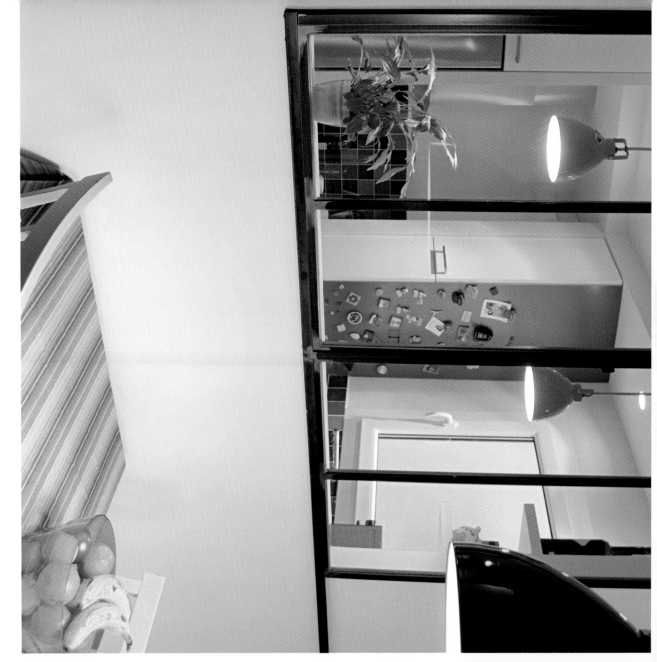

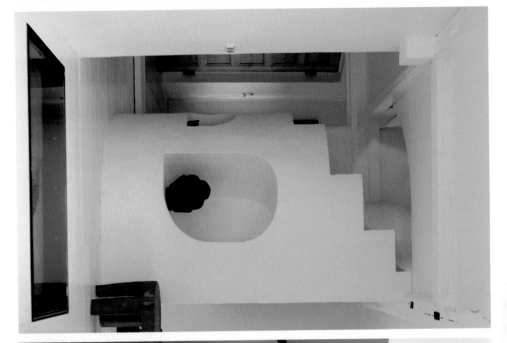

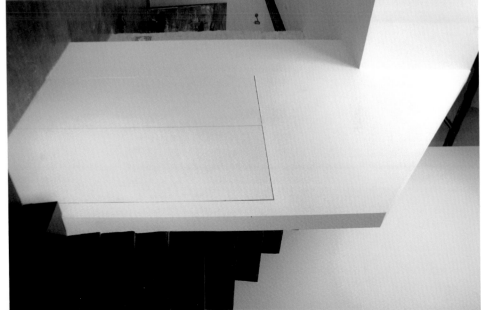

HOME OFFICES

BUREAUX

ARBEITSZIMMER

THUISKANTOREN

L'UFFICIO IN CASA

EL DESPACHO EN CASA

The introduction of new technologies suitable for the home has led to a continuously increasing number of telecommuters. The key to a good home office is to connect professionalism with coziness. Every home office can be unique in style while ensuring a good work place.

Whether it's a small closet, a spare room, or an unused corner of the living room, any space available can become a highly functional home office with the help of a few gallons of paint, smart storage choices, and creative thinking. For that matter, an office at home can simply be two file cabinets and a board across them and give with final touches of the right combination of color, storage and accessories that can greatly enhance the productivity and enjoyment of the space.

A reduced space adapted for working requires special attention to organization in order to carry out the work activities comfortably and efficiently. It is important to keep in mind your specific needs, including storage, desk area, and most importantly, appropriate lighting. When the home office is part of a larger space, it is great to be able to hide any unsightly items in a cabinet or screen the entire home office from the rest of the room with the help of a folding screen, a row of tall plants, or a bookcase. Not because it is work related you should refrain yourself from having fun decorating it. It is your home after all and the rules are your own. Having said this, integrate the office effects with the style of your home by choosing items that look more like furniture than mere office equipment.

L'arrivée de nouvelles technologies adaptées à un usage à domicile ont conduit à une augmentation croissante du nombre de télétravailleurs. Le secret d'un bon espace de travail est de combiner à la fois professionnalisme et confort. Chaque bureau peut être doté d'un style unique tout en procurant un bon espace de travail.

Qu'il s'agisse d'un petit placard, d'une pièce supplémentaire ou d'un coin inutilisé du salon, tout espace disponible peut devenir un bureau très fonctionnel grâce à quelques litres de peinture, des choix de rangements astucieux et un peu de créativité. Un bureau peut d'ailleurs simplement être constitué de deux classeurs et d'une planche posée dessus. Il suffit de quelques touches finales avec la bonne combinaison de couleurs, de rangements et d'accessoires pour accroître la productivité de l'espace et améliorer la façon dont vous en profiterez.

Un espace réduit, adapté au travail, requiert une attention particulière portée sur l'organisation afin de mener à bien ses activités professionnelles dans le confort et de manière efficace. Il est important de garder à l'esprit vos besoins particuliers, y compris le rangement, la zone de bureau et surtout l'éclairage. Lorsque le bureau fait partie d'un plus grand espace, il est bien de pouvoir cacher tout élément disgracieux dans un placard ou dissimuler l'intégralité du bureau derrière un paravent, une rangée de hautes plantes ou une bibliothèque.

Ce n'est pas parce qu'il est question de travail que vous devez réfréner vos envies de décorations originales. Après tout, il s'agit de votre maison et vous définissez vos propres règles. Ceci dit, il est important d'intégrer vos effets professionnels au style de votre maison en choisissant des éléments ressemblant plus à des meubles qu'à des équipements de bureau.

Die Einführung neuer Technologien hat dazu geführt, dass die Anzahl der Telearbeiter stetig steigt. Der Schlüssel zu einem effektiven Büro im eigenen Zuhause liegt in der optimalen Kombination von Berufsleben und Behaglichkeit. Jedes Home Office kann einen einzigartigen Stil ausstrahlen und gleichzeitig einen komfortablen Arbeitsplatz bieten.

Egal ob es sich um einen Wandschrank, ein freies Zimmer oder eine ungenutzte Ecke im Wohnzimmer handelt - jeder verfügbare Raum kann mithilfe einiger Eimer Farbe, ausgeklügelter Aufbewahrungslösungen und kreativer Ideen in einen praktischen Arbeitsplatz verwandelt werden. Ein Arbeitszimmer kann auch einfach aus zwei Aktenschränken bestehen, über die ein großes Brett als Arbeitsfläche gelegt wird. Mit der richtigen Farbkombination, ausreichend Stauraum und einigen Accessoires wird daraus ein Bereich für produktives Arbeiten mit Spaß.

Bei der Gestaltung eines Arbeitsplatzes auf begrenztem Raum ist darauf zu achten, dass die erforderlichen Tätigkeiten bequem und effizient erledigt werden können. Daher muss auf die individuellen Anforderungen an Stauraum, Arbeitsfläche und - was besonders wichtig ist - die richtige Beleuchtung eingegangen werden. Ist der Arbeitsplatz in einem größeren Zimmer untergebracht, sollte man unansehnliche Gegenstände in einem Schrank verstauen oder den gesamten Arbeitsbereich mithilfe eines Paravents, einer Reihe großer Zimmerpflanzen oder eines Bücherschranks vom Raum abtrennen.

Nur weil das Arbeitszimmer mit dem Arbeitsleben in Verbindung steht, sollte man keineswegs auf den Spaß beim Einrichten und Dekorieren verzichten. Schließlich geht es um Ihr Zuhause - und dort geben Sie allein den Ton an. Gestalten Sie Ihr Home Office also im Einklang mit dem Stil Ihrer Wohnung und wählen Sie schöne Möbelstücke anstelle einer nüchternen Büroausstattung.

De opkomst van nieuwe technologieën in huis heeft ertoe geleid dat het aantal thuiswerkers voortdurend groeit. De manier om een goed thuiskantoor te maken is vakkundigheid met een gezellige ruimte te combineren. Elk thuiskantoor kan uniek in stijl en tegelijkertijd een goede werkplek zijn.

Of het nu om een kleine studeerkamer, een extra vertrek of een ongebruikte hoek van de woonkamer gaat, elke beschikbare ruimte kan veranderen in een zeer functioneel thuiskantoor met behulp van wat verf, een intelligent opbergsysteem en een creatieve denkwijze. Wat dat betreft kan een kantoor aan huis simpelweg bestaan uit twee archiefkasten met een bord ertussen waaraan een finishing touch wordt gegeven met de juiste kleurencombinatie, opbergsystemen en accessoires die in staat zijn om de productiviteit en het genieten van de ruimte enorm te bevorderen. Een kleine voor het werk aangepaste ruimte moet optimaal ingericht worden om het werk comfortabel en efficiënt te kunnen uitvoeren. Het is belangrijk om rekening te houden met uw specifieke behoeften, met inbegrip van opbergruimte, een bureauzone en, nog belangrijker, een geschikte verlichting. Wanneer het thuiskantoor deel uitmaakt van een grotere ruimte, dan is het een goed idee om lelijke voorwerpen in een kast te verbergen of de gehele werkplek af te schermen met een kamerscherm, een rij hoge planten of een boekenkast.

Het moet niet zo zijn dat u zich moet intomen bij de decoratie omdat het om een werkruimte gaat. Het is immers uw huis en u bepaalt de regels. U kunt de kantoorelementen ook opnemen in de stijl van uw woning door te kiezen voor voorwerpen die meer op huiselijk dan op kantoormeubilair lijken.

L'arrivo in casa delle nuove tecnologie ha fatto sì che il numero di persone che svolgono il telelavoro si sia moltiplicato in modo esponenziale. La chiave per disporre di un buon ufficio in casa è combinare professionalità e uno spazio accogliente. Ogni ufficio può avere uno stile unico e nel contempo fornire un luogo adatto in cui lavorare. Che si tratti di un piccolo studio, di una stanza libera o di un angolo non utilizzato in salotto, qualsiasi spazio può accogliere un ufficio funzionale e un tocco di creatività. Infatti un ufficio in casa può essere composto semplicemente da un paio di mobili in cui archiviare i documenti, una lavagna sistemata tra questi e il tocco finale che rappresenta la combinazione perfetta tra colore, contenimento e accessori, per stimolare al massimo la produttività e l'utilizzo dello spazio.

Qualsiasi spazio ridotto adattato per uso professionale deve essere organizzato in modo ottimale per consentire lo svolgimento dell'attività lavorativa in modo comodo ed efficiente. È importante tenere conto delle necessità specifiche, comprese quelle di contenimento, della presenza di una scrivania e soprattutto di un'illuminazione adeguata. Quando l'ufficio si inserisce in una stanza più ampia, è consigliabile nascondere gli oggetti antiestetici in un mobile o isolare l'intero angolo ufficio dietro un paravento, una fila di piante alte o una libreria.

Il fatto però che si tratti di uno spazio di lavoro non significa che si debba rinunciare al gusto di arredarlo. In fin dei conti, la casa è di chi vi vive e ognuno definisce al suo interno le proprie regole. Detto questo, si consiglia di integrare l'ufficio con lo stile della casa selezionando oggetti più simili a elementi di arredo che da ufficio.

La incorporación de las nuevas tecnologías en los hogares ha hecho que el número de personas con teletrabajo se multiplique exponencialmente. La clave para disfrutar de un buen despacho en casa es combinar profesionalidad con un espacio acogedor. Cada despacho puede presentar un estilo único y, a la par, proporcionar un buen lugar de trabajo.

Ya se trate de un pequeño gabinete, de una habitación libre o de un rincón desaprovechado del salón, cualquier espacio puede acoger un despacho funcional con la ayuda de un poco de pintura, algún que otro mueble organizador inteligente y pensamiento creativo. De hecho, un despacho en casa puede constar simplemente de un par de armarios archivadores con una pizarra entre ellos y ese toque final que aporta la combinación idónea de color, almacenaje y accesorios capaz de estimular enormemente la productividad y el disfrute del espacio.

Todo espacio reducido adaptado para trabajar debe estar organizado de manera óptima para poder desempeñar la actividad laboral con comodidad y eficiencia. Es importante tener en cuenta las necesidades específicas, incluidos el almacenaje, la zona del escritorio y, sobre todo, una iluminación apropiada. Cuando el despacho se inscribe en una estancia más amplia, es recomendable ocultar los objetos antiestéticos en un armario o apantallar todo el despacho tras un biombo, una hilera de plantas altas o una librería.

Ahora bien, el hecho de que sea un espacio para trabajar no implica tener que refrenarse de divertirse decorándolo. Al fin y al cabo, es nuestra casa y somos nosotros quienes establecemos las reglas. Dicho esto, integraremos los efectos de la oficina con el estilo del hogar seleccionando objetos más similares a mobiliario que a equipamiento de oficina.

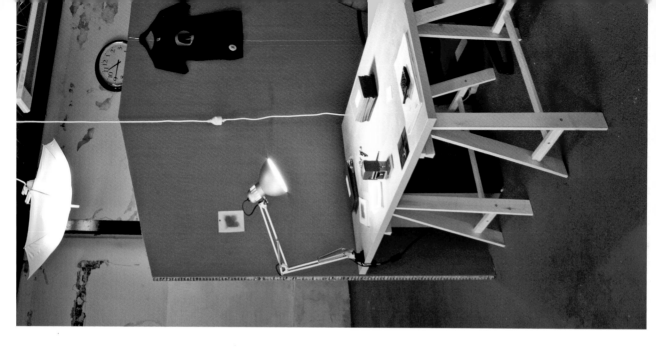

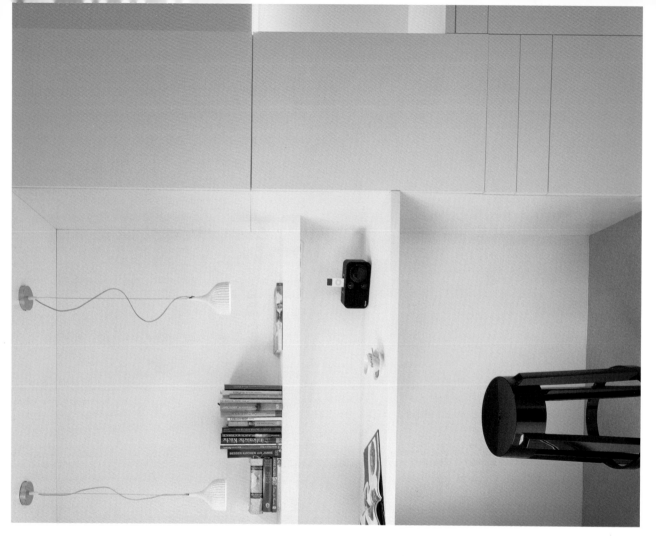

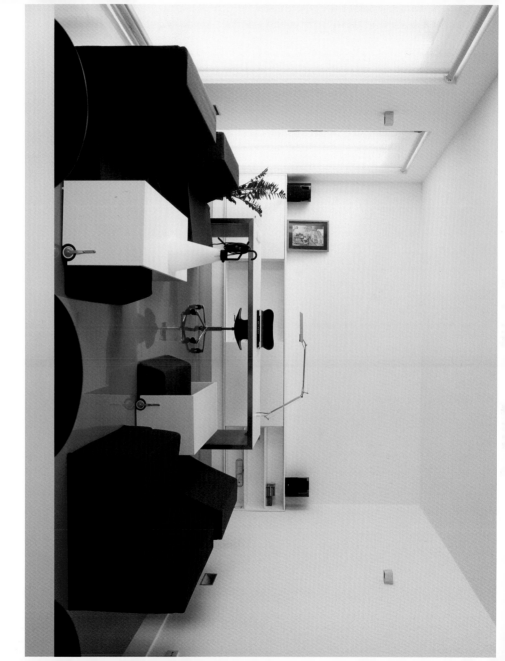

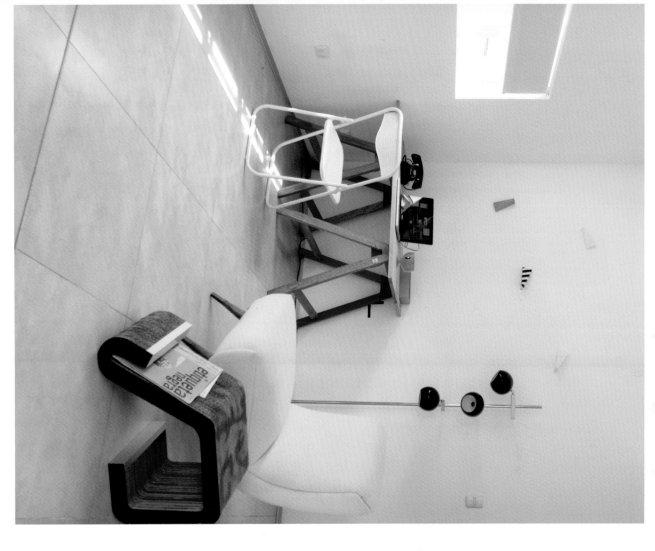

LIVING ROOMS

SALLES DE SÉJOUR

WOHNZIMMER

WOONKAMERS

SALOTTO

SALONES

Auch in einem winzigen Essbereich kann ein erlesenes Menü serviert werden. Unabhängig von der Größe des Raumes ist es jedoch stets wichtig, bestimmte Bereiche in den Mittelpunkt zu rücken und Ess- und Wohnbereich voneinander zu trennen bzw. zu kombinieren. In den meisten Fällen ist das Wohnzimmer – insbesondere in kleinen Wohnungen – der Raum, in dem sich die meisten Aktivitäten abspielen. Bevor man sich der Dekoration und Anordnung der Möbel widmet, muss daher geklärt werden, wozu das Wohnzimmer dienen soll, z. B. zum Essen, Fernsehen, Musik hören, Lesen und zur Unterhaltung. Anschließend kann man entsprechend entscheiden, welche Möbel (sofern noch nicht vorhanden) benötigt werden.

Um einzelne Zonen innerhalb des Raumes hervorzuheben, können Sie sich an architektonischen Elementen (z. B. Kamin oder Fenster) oder auch an einem zentralen Möbelstück (z. B. Sofa oder Esstisch) orientieren. Sehr wahrscheinlich ergeben sich automatisch mehrere Bereiche. Versuchen Sie in diesem Fall, einen Bezugspunkt besonders in den Vordergrund zu rücken anstatt diverse Bereiche miteinander konkurrieren zu lassen. Im nächsten Schritt werden die Möbel in den einzelnen Bereichen arrangiert. Achten Sie bei der Festlegung der Standorte für die einzelnen Möbelstücke darauf, dass freie Wege durch den Raum geschaffen werden. Danach geht es darum, den Raum mit Wohnaccessoires auszustatten. Beginnen Sie auch hier mit den einzelnen Bereichen, die Aufmerksamkeit erregen: platzieren Sie dort Ihre Lieblingsstücke. Denken Sie daran, dass durch die Gruppierung mehrerer Gegenstände in aufeinander abgestimmten Farben eine stärkere optische Wirkung erzielt wird als durch die separate Aufstellung einzelner Objekte.

Even a tiny dining room can serve-up big style. Regardless of the size though, the critical issue is creating focal points and delimit or not the sitting area and the dining area. The living room is in most cases, and most particularly when dealing with a reduced space, the room in the house where most activities take place. Before taking any decoration decision and arranging furniture, be clear about what activities will take place in the living room: eating, watching TV, listening to music, reading, entertaining, etc. This will determine the type of furniture you will need if you do not have them yet.

Creating a focal point around an activity can be just as simple as an architectural feature in the room such as a fireplace or a window, or a particular piece of furniture such as a sofa or a dining table. Chances are that you end up with more than one focal point. If this occurs, try to emphasize one over the other as to not create competing focal points. Once you have these defined, the next step will consist of arranging the furniture around the focal points. While assigning a place to each piece of furniture, try to define paths through the room and keep them clear. All is left to do is accessorizing the rooms. These are the areas in the room that attract most attention, so use the items you like the best and let them take center stage in the room. Remember that grouping items of harmonizing colors create greater effect than if they are displayed separately).

Même une petite salle à manger peut avoir beaucoup de style. Sans tenir compte de la taille, l'essentiel est de créer différents points focaux et de séparer ou non le coin salon de la salle à manger. La salle de séjour est dans la majorité des cas, et plus particulièrement lorsqu'il s'agit d'espaces réduits, la pièce de la maison dans laquelle se déroulent la plupart des activités. Avant de prendre toute décision concernant la décoration ou l'agencement du mobilier, il est important de savoir comment la salle de séjour sera utilisée : pour manger, regarder la télé, écouter de la musique, lire, se divertir, etc. Cela vous aidera à déterminer le genre de meubles dont vous avez besoin si vous n'en avez pas encore.

Créer un point focal autour d'une activité en particulier peut être très simple, à l'aide, par exemple, d'un détail architectural tel qu'une cheminée ou une fenêtre, ou encore grâce à un meuble comme un canapé ou une table à manger. Il est même probable que vous obteniez plusieurs points focaux. Dans ce cas, n'essayez pas de mettre l'accent sur l'un d'entre eux, afin de ne pas créer de concurrence. Une fois les points focaux définis, la prochaine étape consistera à agencer les meubles autour de ces derniers. Au moment d'attribuer une place à chacun de vos meubles, essayez de délimiter des chemins de passage dans la pièce et de les laisser dégagés. Tout ce qu'il restera à faire ensuite est de personnaliser les pièces. Pour cela, commencez par les points focaux. Ceux-ci sont les zones de la pièce qui attirent le regard en premier, alors placez-y les objets que vous préférez et laissez-les jouer le rôle principal. N'oubliez pas que le regroupement d'objets de couleurs harmonieuses créé un meilleur effet que s'ils sont disposés séparément.

Zelfs een kleine zitkamer kan zeer stijlvol zijn. Ongeacht de grootte is het fundamenteel om middelpunten te creëren en de zit- en eethoek al dan niet af te bakenen. De woonkamer is meestal, met name als het om een kleine ruimte gaat, het vertrek in huis waar de meeste activiteiten plaatsvinden. Voordat er een besluit over de decoratie en inrichting wordt genomen, moet men duidelijk voor ogen hebben welke activiteiten er in de woonkamer zullen plaatsvinden. Bijvoorbeeld eten, tv kijken, muziek luisteren, lezen en vermaak. Dit bepaalt het type meubilair dat u nodig zult hebben als u het nog niet heeft.

Het creëren van een middelpunt rondom een activiteit kan net zo eenvoudig zijn als het in het oog laten vallen van een architectonisch element van de kamer, zoals een open haard of een raam, of van een bepaald meubelstuk, zoals een bank of eettafel. Waarschijnlijk zult u uiteindelijk meer dan één middelpunt hebben. Is dit het geval, probeer dan één element boven het andere uit te laten springen, zodat er geen wedijverende brandpunten ontstaan. Nadat u het middelpunt heeft vastgesteld, moeten de meubels er omheen worden opgesteld. Als alle meubels een plaats hebben toegekend, probeer dan loopruimte door de kamer af te bakenen en vrij te houden. Nu hoeft de kamer enkel nog te worden voorzien van accessoires. Begin met de middelpunten. Dit zijn de delen van de kamer die de meeste aandacht trekken. Gebruik dan ook elementen die u het mooist vindt en geef ze een belangrijke rol in het vertrek. Denk eraan dat het groeperen van voorwerpen met harmonieuze kleuren een beter effect sorteert dan ze van elkaar gescheiden op te stellen.

Persino un salotto di piccole dimensioni può presentarsi in grande stile. Al di là delle dimensioni, è fondamentale creare punti focali e scegliere se delimitare o meno la zona tinello da quella dedicata al relax. Come regola generale, il salotto – soprattutto quando occupa uno spazio ridotto – è l'ambiente in cui si svolge la maggior parte delle attività. Prima di prendere una decisione su come arredarlo o decorarlo, è necessario analizzare quali attività vi vengono svolte. Alcuni esempi: mangiare, guardare la TV, ascoltare la musica, leggere, trascorrere del tempo insieme.

Questo determinerà il tipo di arredamento necessario, se ancora non è disponibile. Creare un punto focale intorno a una data attività può risultare tanto semplice quanto mettere in risalto un elemento architettonico: un caminetto o una finestra o ancora un mobile (un divano o un tavolo da pranzo). È abbastanza probabile che vengano a crearsi più punti focali. In tal caso, è bene concentrarsi su uno in particolare affinché non si crei competizione tra i vari elementi. Una volta definiti questi punti di riferimento, sistemare il resto dei mobili intorno ad essi. Quando si assegna un posto a un mobile, occorre definire dei ipercorsi nella stanza e mantenerli liberi. A questo punto mancano solo gli accessori. Iniziare dai punti focali. Queste sono le zone che catturano maggiormente l'attenzione; qui sarà possibile disporvi gli oggetti che più piacciono, lasciando a loro il ruolo di protagonisti nell'ambiente. È importante ricordare che il raggruppamento di colori armonici crea un effetto migliore rispetto a esporli separatamente.

Incluso un salón diminuto puede lucir un gran estilo. Al margen de sus dimensiones, lo fundamental es crear puntos focales y optar entre delimitar o no las zonas de comedor y de relax. Por regla general, el salón, sobre todo cuando ocupa un espacio reducido, es la estancia que acoge la mayor parte de las actividades de un hogar. Antes de adoptar una decisión en cuanto a su decoración y mobiliario, conviene analizar qué actividades se desempeñarán en él; por ejemplo: comer, ver la televisión, escuchar música, leer y compartir el ocio. Esto determinará el tipo de mobiliario necesario, si aún no se dispone de él.

Crear un punto focal en torno a una actividad puede resultar tan sencillo como destacar bien un elemento arquitectónico de la estancia (una chimenea o una ventana), bien un mueble (un sofá o una mesa de comedor). Es bastante probable que acabe teniendo varios puntos focales. Si esto ocurriese, puede realzarse uno por encima de los demás para que no se establezcan competencias. Una vez definidos estos focos, se coloca el resto de los muebles alrededor de ellos. Al asignar un lugar a un mueble, hay que definir rutas a través de la estancia y mantenerlas despejadas. Lo único que queda ahora es añadir los accesorios. Empezaremos por los puntos focales. Son las zonas que más atraen la atención, de manera que dispondremos en ellas los adornos que más nos gusten y les dejaremos adoptar el papel protagonista de la estancia, sin olvidar que agrupar objetos de colores armoniosos crea un mejor efecto que exponerlos por separado.

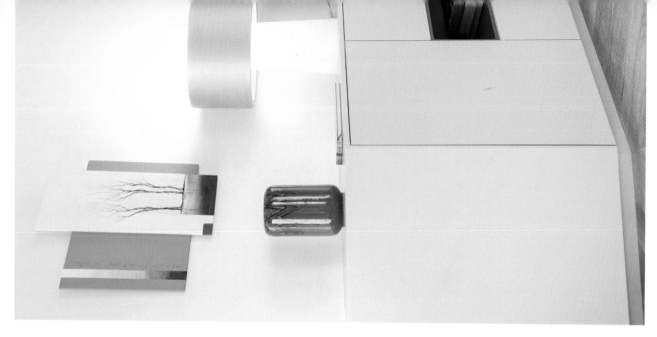

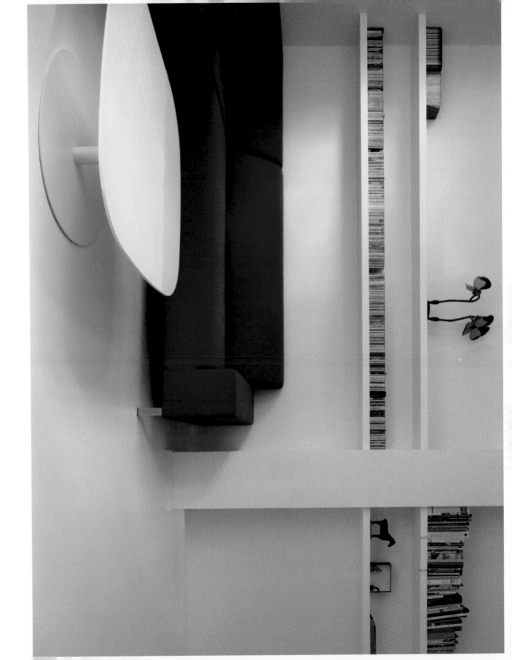

138

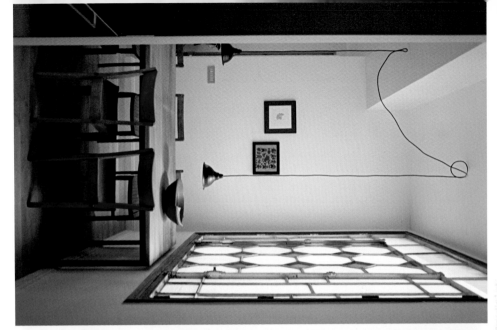

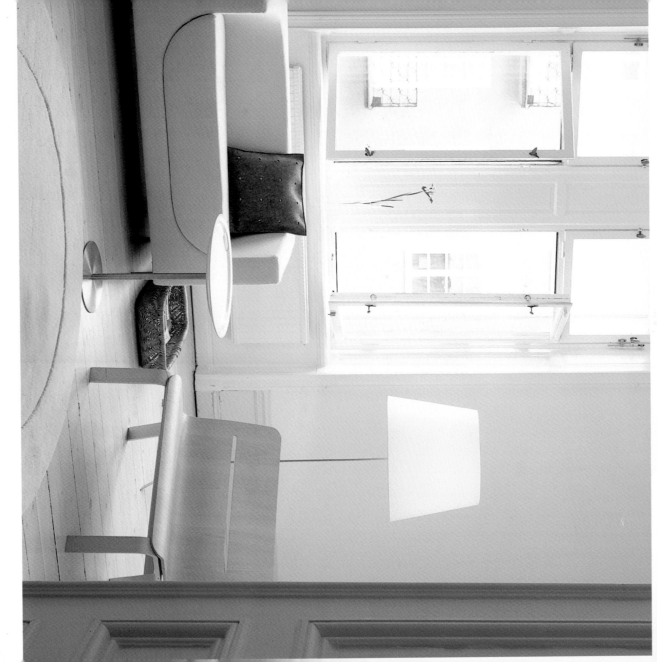

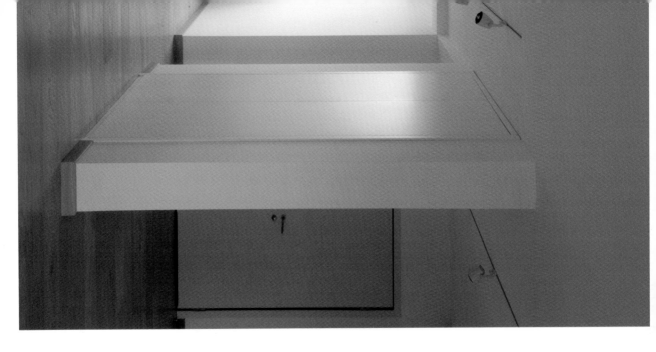

151

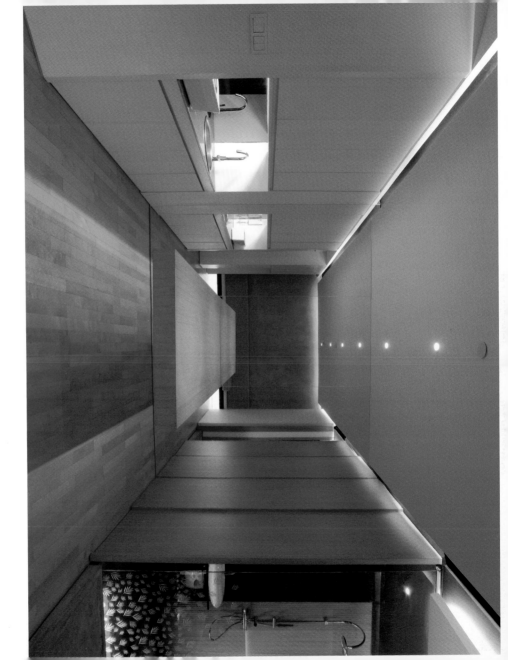

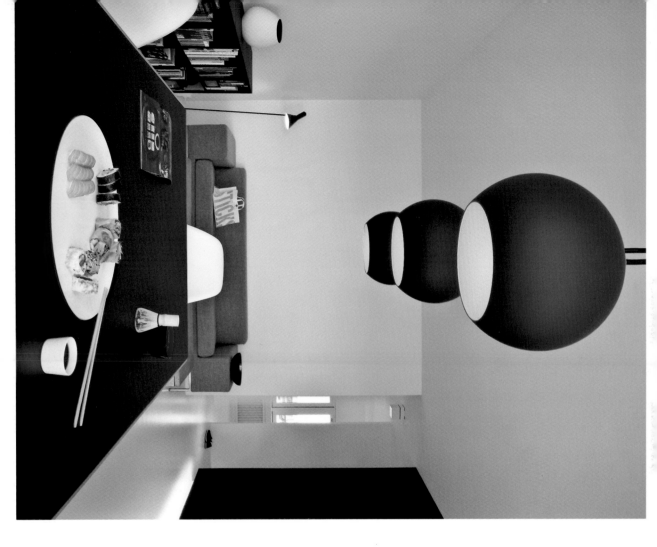

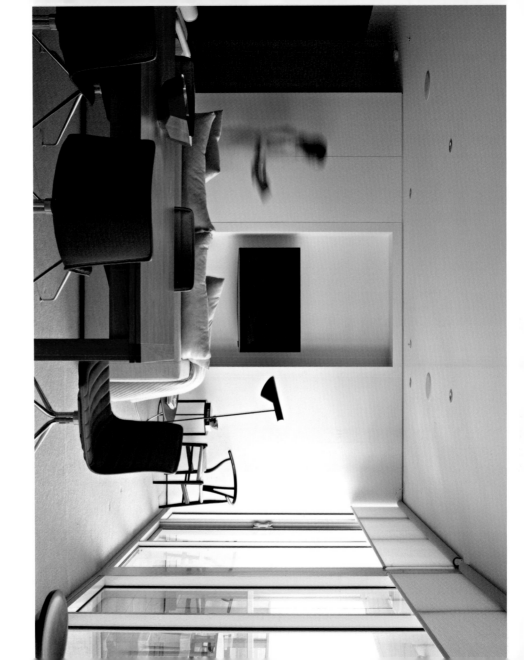

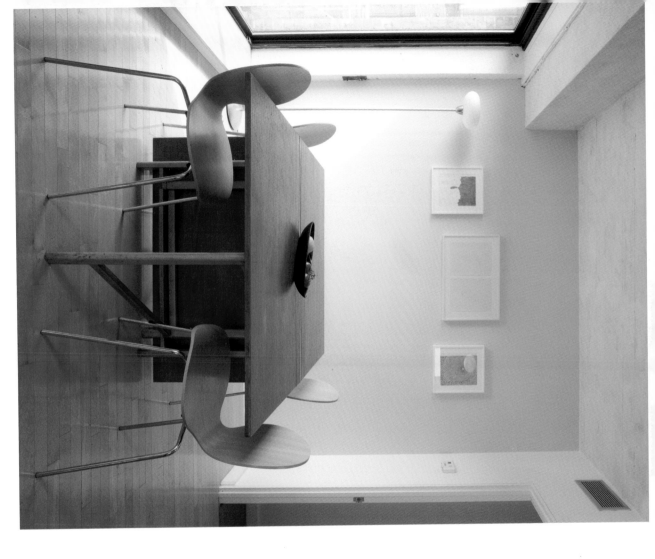

KITCHENS

CUISINES

KÜCHE

KEUKENS

CUCINA

COCINAS

The kitchen is the room in the house that represents the biggest challenge whether it is a new construction or a remodel. It has most closely followed human evolution and has been adapted to evolving needs and lifestyles. While traditional kitchens were solely utilitarian spaces, hidden away and intended to be used only by the homemaker, now even the tiniest kitchen tuck away in a corner has pride of place in the household and is integral to the living and entertaining areas. A well planned kitchen saves time and facilitates the tasks that involve storage, food preparation, cooking and washing. While a small kitchen may not be suited for gourmet cooking, it could still be a superb example of efficiency.

When the space is limited it is best to use light colors and use accent tones to create focal areas. Cabinet makers and equipment manufacturers offer a wide variety of finishes suitable for every taste.

Cabinetry usually makes up the visually largest block in the kitchen. Consider the varied sizes and shapes such as wall cabinets, base cabinets and floor to ceiling cabinets. Countertops and backsplashes are also an important visual element. Of course, there are the floors, the walls and the ceiling. Special effort should be put into maximizing the work space. Highly functional organizing devices that complement storage units help you unclutter your cabinets. Hang a pot rack to give yourself some more cabinet space. This solution seems to be a popular look in many decorating styles.

La cuisine est la pièce de la maison qui représente le plus grand défi, qu'il s'agisse d'une nouvelle construction ou d'une rénovation. Elle a suivi de très près l'évolution humaine en s'adaptant aux besoins et modes de vie changeants. Autrefois, les cuisines traditionnelles n'étaient que des espaces fonctionnels, placés à l'abri des regards et destinés à n'être utilisés que par la maîtresse de maison. Aujourd'hui, même la plus petite cuisine casée dans un coin occupe une place d'honneur dans le foyer et fait partie intégrante des espaces de vie et de divertissement. Une cuisine bien agencée permet de gagner du temps et de faciliter les tâches relatives au stockage, à la cuisine et au nettoyage. Bien qu'une petite cuisine ne soit pas adaptée à la pratique de la haute gastronomie, elle peut tout de même être un modèle d'efficacité.

Lorsque l'espace est limité, la meilleure chose à faire est d'utiliser des couleurs claires et des teintes plus prononcées afin de mettre l'accent sur certaines zones. Les ébénistes et fabricants de matériaux proposent une grande variété de finitions adaptées à tous les goûts.

L'ébénisterie occupe généralement la plus grande place dans une cuisine, avec différentes formes et différentes tailles, que ce soit sur les murs, au sol ou au plafond. Les plans de travail et dosserets sont également des éléments visuels très importants. Bien sûr, il y a aussi les sols, les murs et le plafond. Il est essentiel de tout faire pour optimiser l'espace de travail. Des systèmes de rangement hautement fonctionnels permettant de compléter les unités de stockage peuvent vous aider à faire de la place dans vos placards. Vous pouvez par exemple accrocher un porte-casseroles pour gagner de la place. Cette solution semble avoir du succès dans de nombreux styles de décoration.

Die Küche ist der Raum, der in jedem Zuhause – sei es im Rahmen eines Neubaus oder bei einer Umgestaltung – die größte Herausforderung darstellt. Küchen haben sich genau wie der Mensch kontinuierlich weiterentwickelt und wurden an die sich verändernden Bedürfnisse und Lebensweisen angepasst. Während man eine Küche früher ausschließlich unter funktionellen Gesichtspunkten gestaltete, sie regelrecht in der Wohnung versteckt wurde und meist nur die Hausfrau sie nutzte, behauptet heutzutage auch die kleinste Küche, die in einer winzigen Ecke untergebracht ist, ihren stolzen Platz im Haushalt und ist ein fester Bestandteil des Wohnbereichs. Eine gut geplante Küche spart Zeit und erleichtert die Arbeiten rund um Aufbewahrung, Vorbereitung der Zutaten, Kochen und Abwaschen. Eine kleine Küche ist für die Zubereitung von Gourmet-Menüs vielleicht nicht ausreichend, doch sie kann durchaus ein hervorragendes Beispiel für effektives Arbeiten sein.

In kleineren Räumen sollte man helle Farben verwenden und kräftige Akzente einsetzen, um bestimmte Bereiche hervorzuheben. Die Hersteller von Küchenschränken und Zubehör haben eine breit gefächerte Auswahl an Finishs für jeden Geschmack im Angebot.

Die Küchenschränke spielen in der Küche visuell gesehen die wichtigste Rolle... für die optimale Ausnutzung des vorhandenen Raumes sollte auf die Einrichtung unterschiedlichster Größen und Formen wie z. B. Hängeschränke, Unterschränke und raumhohe Schrankelemente zur Verfügung. Arbeitsflächen und Fliesenspiegel sind ebenso für die optische Wirkung besonders wichtig – und natürlich auch die Bodenbeläge, Wände und Decken. Besonderes Augenmerk sollte auf die Einrichtung möglichst großer Arbeitsflächen gerichtet werden. Praktische Ordnungshelfer tragen dazu bei, den vorhandenen Stauraum optimal zu nutzen. Hängen Sie ein Topfregal auf, um über mehr Platz in den Schränken zu verfügen – eine ansprechende Lösung, die in vielen Einrichtungsstilen eingesetzt werden kann.

De keuken is het vertrek in huis dat de grootste uitdaging is, of het nu om een nieuwe of een verbouwde keuken gaat. Het is de ruimte die de menselijke ontwikkeling van dichtbij heeft gevolgd en zich steeds aan de veranderende behoeften en levensstijlen heeft aangepast. Terwijl traditionele keukens louter utilitaire, afgezonderde en voor het gebruik van de huisvrouw bestemde ruimtes waren, nemen tegenwoordig zelfs de kleinste in een hoek weggestopte keukens een eervolle plaats in huis in en maken volledig deel uit van woonen ontspanningsruimten. Een goed georganiseerde keuken bespaart tijd en vereenvoudigt taken zoals opbergen, eten bereiden, koken en afwassen. Hoewel een kleine keuken wellicht niet geschikt is voor de bereiding van culinaire hoogstandjes, kan deze ruimte wel een voortreffelijk voorbeeld van efficiëntie zijn.

Wanneer de ruimte beperkt is, kunnen het beste lichte kleuren worden toegepast en dienen fellere tinten te worden gebruikt om de opvallende zones in het oog te laten springen. Fabrikanten van kasten en andere uitrustingen bieden voor elke smaak een afwerking. Normaal gesproken zijn de keukenkasten de opvallendste elementen van de keuken. Neem de verschillende formaten en vormen voor onderkasten, bovenkasten en kasten van vloer tot plafond in beschouwing. Aanrechtbladen en backsplashes zijn eveneens opvallende elementen. Natuurlijk zijn er ook de vloeren, wanden en het plafond. Het belangrijkst is een zo groot mogelijk werkoppervlak te creëren. Ook zijn er zeer functionele ladeverdelers en rekjes waardoor kasten nog beter opgeruimd en netjes gehouden kunnen worden. Breng een pannenrek aan om over wat meer kastruimte te beschikken. Deze oplossing lijkt in vele decoratiestijlen populair te worden.

La cucina è l'ambiente della casa che pone maggiori difficoltà, sia nel caso di un nuovo edificio che di una ristrutturazione. Si tratta dell'ambiente che maggiormente ha seguito l'evoluzione umana adattandosi a necessità e a stili di vita sempre diversi. Mentre le cucine di un tempo erano spazi meramente funzionali, nascosti e destinati all'uso esclusivo della donna di casa, oggi anche le cucine più piccole e anguste occupano un posto d'onore nella casa e sono parte integrante delle zone destinate al relax e alla vita sociale. Una cucina ben organizzata consente di risparmiare tempo e facilita la conservazione degli alimenti, la loro preparazione e cottura nonché il lavaggio dei piatti. È anche se una cucina piccola può non essere l'opzione ideale per un gourmet, può comunque rappresentare un ottimo esempio di efficienza. Quando lo spazio è limitato, conviene usare colori chiari e toni più accattivanti per dare enfasi alle zone di maggiore importanza. I produttori di armadi e altri arredi offrono finiture per tutti i gusti.

Gli elementi in legno sono quelli più visibili in qualsiasi cucina. È importante valutare le forme e le dimensioni per realizzare pensili bassi, a parete e armadiature integrali. I ripiani e i pannelli a parete rappresentano degli elementi visivi importanti. Vi sono poi il pavimento, le pareti e il soffitto. La cosa più importante è creare la massima superficie di lavoro possibile. Sono disponibili divisori, contenitori, scomparti e cesti per organizzare e tenere in ordine gli oggetti. Per disporre di maggiore spazio nei pensili, è opportuno sistemarvi dei ganci per pentole e coperchi. Questa soluzione sembra aver acquisito popolarità in molti stili decorativi.

La cocina es la estancia de la casa que representa el mayor desafío, tanto si es de nueva construcción como si se remodela. Es la que ha seguido más de cerca la evolución humana y se ha adaptado a las necesidades y los estilos de vida cambiantes. Mientras que las cocinas tradicionales eran espacios meramente utilitarios, recónditos y destinados a un uso exclusivo por parte del ama de casa, ahora incluso las cocinas más diminutas ocupan un lugar de honor en la vivienda y forman parte integral de las zonas destinadas al ocio. Una cocina bien organizada ahorra tiempo y facilita las tareas de guardar los alimentos, prepararlos, cocinarnos y fregar los platos. Y si bien una cocina pequeña puede no ser la opción ideal para un gourmet, sí puede suponer un magnífico ejemplo de eficiencia. Cuando el espacio es limitado, conviene usar colores claros y tonos más llamativos para acentuar las zonas más destacadas. Los fabricantes de armarios y otro equipamiento ofrecen acabados para todos los gustos.

La carpintería es el elemento más visible en cualquier cocina, por lo que deben sopesarse las formas y los tamaños adecuados para armarios bajos, armarios de pared y armarios integrales. Las encimeras y los paneles de pared constituyen asimismo elementos visuales importantes. Por supuesto, también están los suelos, las paredes y el techo. Lo principal es generar la máxima superficie de trabajo posible. Existen también organizadores, carruseles y cestos que permiten tener los armarios organizados y despejados. Instalar un colgador de ollas permite disponer de más espacio en los armarios, una solución que parece haber cobrado popularidad en muchos estilos de decoración.

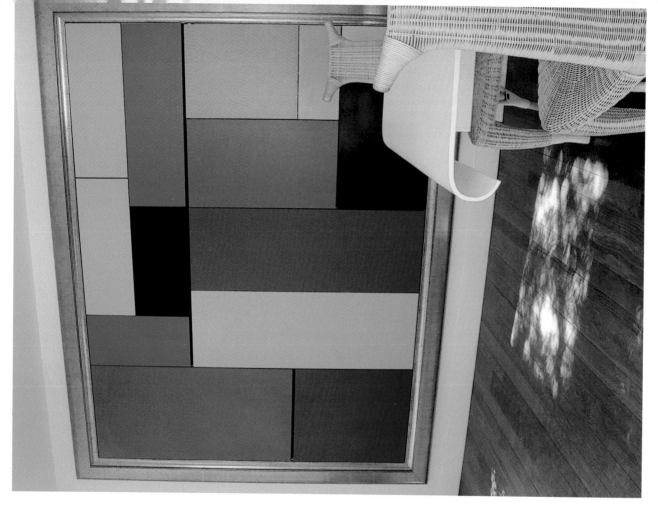

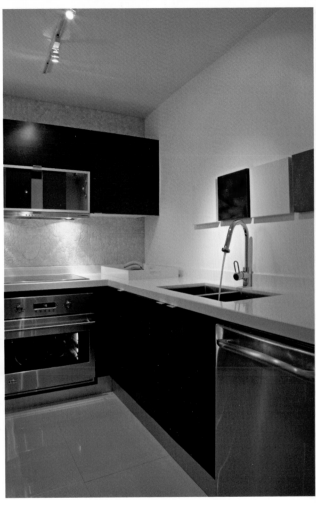

BEDROOMS

CHAMBRES

SCHLAFZIMMER

SLAAPKAMERS

CAMERA DA LETTO

DORMITORIOS

Being the most personal of rooms in the apartment, the bedroom presents an opportunity to experiment and accessorize. This space allows just as much flexibility as any other room in regards to color and style, making decoration opportunities almost endless. It could be anything that strikes your fancy: a cozy nest, an elegant retreat from the world outside, or a museum filled with personal objects. But regardless, the atmosphere created should be comforting and relaxing. Fabrics, used for curtains, throw pillows, bedspreads, sheets and upholstery are a good way to make the bedroom feel and look comfortable, and also can express your tastes and personality. Be aware that these fabrics occupy a large visual surface in the bedroom. The design approach depends on the intended use of the room. If the room is a mere place to sleep, you will probably take a different approach than if it is also used as a home office. In that case, and for your own sake, try to establish some rules such as no laptops in bed. Working from home should not result in the home office taking over your bedroom.

I am so not in favor of sharing the bedroom with the home office that I would suggest you resort to the classic guestroom-home office combo if you have this opportunity. This solution seems to make more sense since the guest bedroom is only occupied sporadically and become more functional by using it for another purpose. This option makes sense, of course, only if your guests do not stay for long period.

S'agissant de la pièce la plus personnelle de l'appartement, la chambre peut être l'occasion d'expérimenter et d'accessoiriser. Cet espace permet tout autant de flexibilité que les autres pièces en termes de couleur et de style, avec des possibilités de décoration infinies. Chacun peut avoir différentes envies : un petit nid douillet, une retraite élégante du monde extérieur ou encore un musée rempli d'objets personnels. Quoi qu'il en soit, l'atmosphère créée doit être agréable et relaxante. Des tissus, utilisés pour les rideaux, des coussins, des dessus-de-lit, des draps et différents tissus d'ameublement peuvent être un bon moyen de donner à la chambre une allure et un ressenti confortable, ainsi que d'exprimer vos goûts et votre personnalité. Soyez conscient que ces tissus occupent une vaste surface visuelle dans la chambre.

L'approche stylistique dépend de la façon dont vous souhaitez utiliser la chambre. Si celle-ci est simplement un endroit pour dormir, vous aurez probablement une approche différente que si elle faisait également office de bureau. Dans ce dernier cas, et pour votre bien-être, essayez de mettre en place quelques règles, comme pas d'ordinateur sur le lit. Travailler à domicile ne devrait pas avoir pour conséquence une chambre envahie par le bureau.

Je n'encouragerais pas d'utiliser la même pièce pour le bureau et la chambre, et je suggèrerais plutôt d'avoir recours à la combinaison classique chambre d'amis/bureau, si vous en avez l'opportunité. Cette solution est plus logique car la chambre d'amis n'est occupée qu'occasionnellement et devient donc plus fonctionnelle si vous lui attribuez un autre usage. Toutefois, cette option n'est possible que si vos invités ne restent pas pour une longue période.

Das Schlafzimmer ist der persönlichste Bereich eines Zuhauses und bietet daher die Möglichkeit zum Experimentieren sowie zum Dekorieren mit den unterschiedlichsten Wohnaccessoires. Da wie in allen anderen Zimmern jeder gewünschte Farbton und Einrichtungsstil möglich ist, können unzählige Einrichtungsideen umgesetzt werden. Das Schlafzimmer kann genau das sein, was Sie sich wünschen: ein behagliches Nest, ein eleganter Ort, um sich von der Außenwelt zurückzuziehen, oder ein Museum voller persönlicher Gegenstände. Unabhängig davon, für welche Option Sie sich entscheiden, sollte Ihr Schlafzimmer stets behaglich eingerichtet sein und zum Ausruhen und Entspannen einladen. Vorhangstoffe, Zierkissen, Tagesdecken, Bettwäsche und Polsterstoffe in den verschiedensten Ausführungen lassen ein Schlafzimmer wohnlich wirken und drücken gleichzeitig den Geschmack und persönlichen Stil der Bewohner aus. Denken Sie bei der Auswahl stets daran, dass diese Stoffe im Schlafzimmer eine große Fläche einnehmen.

Die gewählte Einrichtung hängt davon ab, welche Funktionen das Schlafzimmer erfüllt. Dient es ausschließlich zum Schlafen, wird die Gestaltung anders aussehen, als wenn es außerdem ein Home Office beherbergen soll. In letzterem Fall sollten Sie um Ihres Wohlbefindens willen bestimmte Regeln aufstellen (z. B. „Kein Laptop im Bett"). Sorgen Sie dafür, dass das Schlafzimmer nicht von der Arbeit beherrscht wird. Da ich jedoch grundsätzlich dagegen bin, einen Arbeitsplatz im Schlafzimmer unterzubringen, schlage ich vor, auf die klassische Kombination „Gästezimmer mit Heimarbeitsplatz" zurückzugreifen, falls diese Möglichkeit besteht. Diese Lösung ist weitaus praktischer, da das Gästezimmer nur gelegentlich belegt ist und durch den Arbeitsplatz eine zusätzliche Funktion erfüllt. Diese Option ist natürlich nur dann sinnvoll, wenn Sie Gäste nicht für einen längeren Zeitraum beherbergen.

Aangezien de slaapkamer het meest persoonlijke vertrek van de woning is, heeft u hier een voortreffelijke gelegenheid om met de decoratie te experimenteren. Deze ruimte biedt net zoveel flexibiliteit als elke andere kamer wat betreft kleur en stijl, waardoor er ontelbaar veel mogelijkheden zijn. U kunt ervan maken wat u wilt: een gezellig nest, een elegante plek om u terug te trekken van de buitenwereld of een museum vol persoonlijke voorwerpen. Maar ongeacht de optie waarvoor u kiest, de gecreëerde sfeer moet comfortabel en ontspannend zijn. Stoffen, gebruikt voor gordijnen, kussens, beddenspreien, lakens en bekleding, vormen een goede manier om de slaapkamer er comfortabel uit te laten zien en kunnen eveneens uw smaak en persoonlijkheid uitstralen. Wees er bewust van dat deze stoffen een grote visuele oppervlakte van de slaapkamer in beslag nemen.

De benadering van het design hangt af van de toepassing die u aan het vertrek wilt geven. Als de kamer louter bedoeld is om te slapen, zult u hem waarschijnlijk anders inrichten dan wanneer u hem ook als thuiskantoor gebruikt. In dat geval moet u voor uw eigen belang proberen om een aantal regels op te stellen, zoals geen laptops op bed gebruiken. Thuiswerken mag niet betekenen dat u uw thuiskantoor mee naar de slaapkamer neemt.

In wezen vind ik het geen goed idee dat de slaapkamer en de werkplek dezelfde ruimte delen en stel ik dan ook liever voor dat u een beroep doet op de klassieke combinatie van logeerkamer en werkkamer als u over deze mogelijkheid beschikt. Het gaat om een verstandiger oplossing, aangezien de logeerkamer alleen zo af en toe wordt gebruikt en functioneler is als hij ook een andere bestemming krijgt. Dit alternatief heeft uiteraard alleen zin als uw logees niet voor lange periodes bij u thuis verblijven.

Essendo la stanza più importante della casa, la camera da letto offre l'opportunità di sperimentare negli aspetti decorativi. Questo spazio consente tanta flessibilità quanto qualsiasi altro ambiente in termini di colore e stile, aprendo il campo a soluzioni praticamente infinite. Può così trasformarsi in ciò che più piace a chi lo utilizzerà: un nido accogliente, un elegante rifugio dal mondo esterno o una sorta di museo in cui sono raccolti oggetti personali di ogni tipo. Indipendentemente dall'opzione scelta, l'ambiente dovrà essere confortevole e rilassante. I tessuti per tende, cuscini, coperte, lenzuola e tappezzeria contribuiscono a trasmettere la sensazione e l'aspetto di comodità oltre a esprimere il gusto e la personalità di chi vi vive. È importante ricordare che questi tessuti occupano una grande superficie visiva in camera. L'organizzazione degli spazi dipende dall'uso che si desidera fare della stanza. Se si tratta semplicemente di un luogo in cui dormire, probabilmente si adotterà un approccio diverso rispetto a chi lo utilizza anche come angolo studio o ufficio. In tal caso, per la propria salute, sarà necessario definire alcune regole come ad esempio evitare di utilizzare i computer portatili sul letto. Lavorare da casa non deve significare portarsi il lavoro in camera.

Infatti, sono talmente in disaccordo con l'idea di usare la camera anche come ufficio, che il mio suggerimento è quello di optare per il classico ufficio in casa / stanza degli ospiti, sempre che ve ne sia una. Si tratta di una soluzione più sensata dato che la camera degli ospiti viene occupata solo sporadicamente ed è più funzionale se destinata a un utilizzo aggiuntivo. Logicamente questa alternativa ha significato solo se gli ospiti non si trattengono per periodi particolarmente lunghi!

Por ser la habitación más importante de la vivienda, el dormitorio brinda la oportunidad de experimentar con la decoración. Este espacio permite tanta flexibilidad como cualquier otra estancia en términos de color y estilo, lo cual conlleva unas posibilidades decorativas casi infinitas. Puede ser lo que a uno le apetezca: un nido acogedor, un elegante retiro del mundo exterior o un museo abarrotado de objetos personales. Ahora bien, independientemente de la opción que se elija, el ambiente creado debe ser confortable y relajante. Los tejidos de cortinas, almohadas, colchas, sábanas y tapicería contribuyen a imprimir un aspecto de comodidad, además de expresar nuestros gustos y nuestra personalidad, pero debemos tener en cuenta que estas telas ocupan una gran superficie visual en un dormitorio. El planteamiento del diseño depende del uso que se pretenda dar a la estancia. Si se trata de un mero lugar donde ir a dormir, probablemente adoptará un enfoque distinto que si se va a usarse también como despacho en casa. En tal caso, y por nuestra propia salud, debemos establecer algunas reglas, como no usar ordenadores portátiles en la cama. Trabajar desde casa no debe implicar llevarse el trabajo al dormitorio. De hecho, estoy tan en desacuerdo con la idea de compartir el dormitorio con el despacho que sugeriría recurrir al clásico despacho en casa / habitación de invitados, siempre que baraje esta opción. Se trata de una solución más sensata, puesto que la habitación de invitados se ocupa solo de manera esporádica y resulta más funcional si se destina a un uso adicional. Lógicamente, esta alternativa solo cobra sentido si los invitados no se instalan en casa durante largas temporadas.

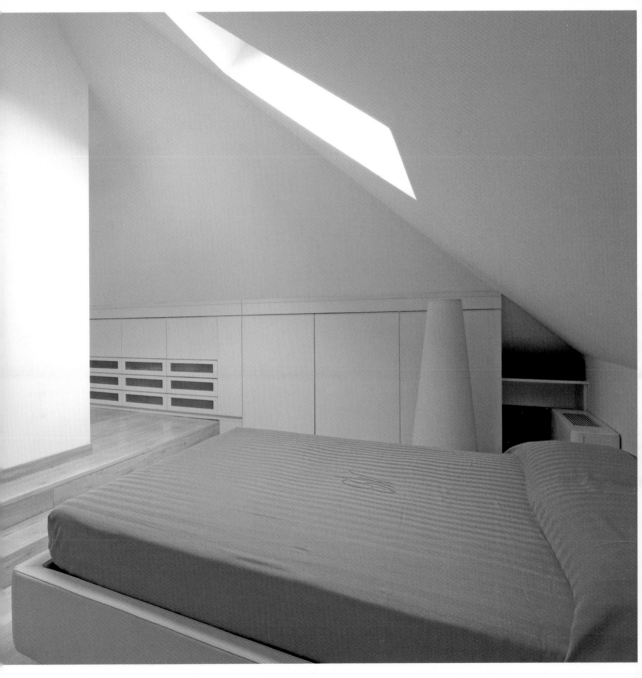

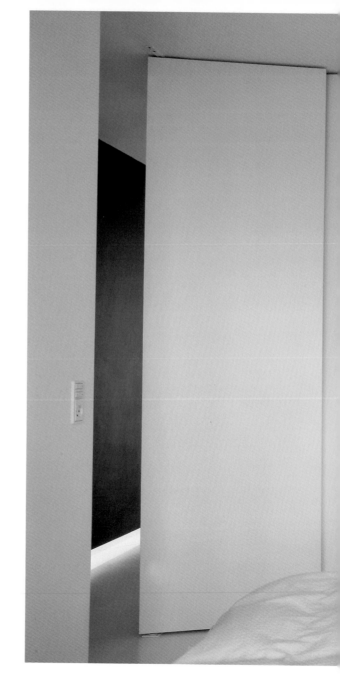

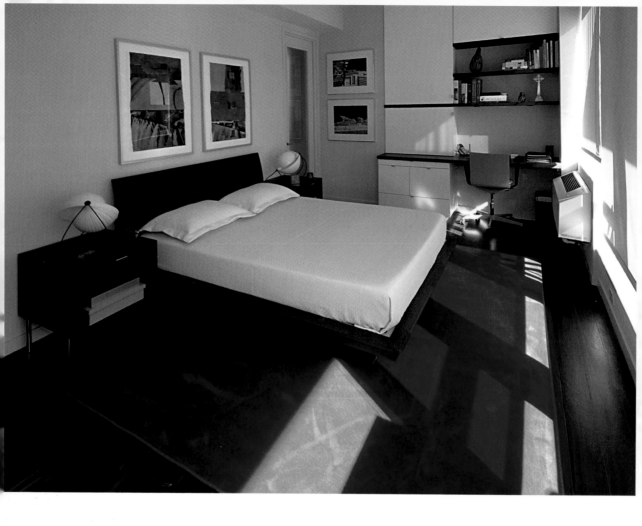

KIDS BEDROOMS

CHAMBRES D'ENFANTS

KINDERZIMMER

KINDERKAMERS

CAMERA DEI BAMBINI

DORMITORIOS INFANTILES

Children's bedrooms are the space they'll spend the most time in whether is for sleeping, for playing or for studying. The central element in the bedroom is, of course, the bed, although a second element will gradually take on increasing importance as the child grows older: the desk or work table. Do not disregard a clear space in the bedroom that will serve as play area. Your kid will appreciate it. If the room is large enough, it will be easier to divide it into different areas. If it is not the case, you will have to resort to furniture that fold away or combine different functions. Special attention should be put into creating an environment with affinity to the child's personality that stimulates curiosity and helps personal development. It is important that the child participates in the decoration of his or her own room. Children may or may not have a clear idea of what they want but they will need you to make an effort to listen and try to understand. Try to make them involved in functional and aesthetic details like the positioning of the bed or the color of the walls. Children relate differently to their environments at different age phases. You know how fast kids grow and so do their personalities. Keep this in mind when designing the room and selecting the furniture. There is the option of buying new furniture as your child grows older or find adaptable furniture, normally more expensive but definitely more useful and cost efficient in the long run.

La chambre est l'endroit dans lequel un enfant passe le plus clair de son temps, que ce soit pour dormir, pour jouer ou pour étudier. L'élément central d'une chambre est bien sûr le lit mais, à mesure que les enfants grandissent, un second élément revêt de plus en plus d'importance : le bureau, ou la table de travail. N'oubliez pas de garder un espace dégagé pour créer une zone de jeu. Votre enfant en sera ravi. Si la pièce est assez grande, il sera plus facile de la diviser en différents espaces. Si tel n'est pas le cas, il faudra avoir recours à des meubles qui peuvent se rabattre ou combiner différentes fonctions. Il est essentiel de concevoir un environnement qui soit en accord avec la personnalité de l'enfant, qui stimule sa curiosité et qui soit favorable à son développement personnel. Il est important que l'enfant participe à la décoration de sa propre chambre. Les enfants peuvent avoir, ou non, une idée précise de ce qu'ils veulent mais il vous faut tout faire pour les écouter et essayer de les comprendre. Essayez de les impliquer dans le choix des détails fonctionnels et esthétiques tels que la position du lit ou la couleur des murs. Selon leur âge, les enfants ont un rapport différent avec leur environnement.
Comme vous le savez, les enfants grandissent très vite et leur personnalité change. Gardez cela à l'esprit au moment de concevoir le design de la pièce et de choisir les meubles. Vous avez la possibilité d'acheter des nouveaux meubles à mesure que votre enfant grandit, ou de trouver des meubles adaptables. Ces derniers sont plus chers mais ils sont assurément plus utiles et rentables sur le long terme.

Das Kinderzimmer ist der Raum, in dem die Kleinen am meisten Zeit verbringen, sei es zum Schlafen, zum Spielen oder zum Lernen. Das zentrale Elemente im Kinderzimmer ist selbstverständlich das Bett, wobei ein zweiter Aspekt mit zunehmendem Alter des Kindes immer wichtiger wird: der Schreibtisch. Achten Sie auch darauf, dass es eine freie Fläche im Kinderzimmer gibt, die als Spielbereich dienen kann... Ihr Kind wird es Ihnen danken! Ist das Zimmer groß genug, ist die Aufteilung in verschiedene Bereiche recht einfach. Bei kleineren Zimmern bietet es sich an, auf Klappmöbel oder Möbelstücke mit mehreren Funktionen zurückzugreifen. Es sollte viel Wert darauf gelegt werden, eine Umgebung zu schaffen, die der Persönlichkeit des Kindes gerecht wird, seine Neugier und Fantasie anregt und seine Entwicklung fördert. Besonders wichtig ist, dass Sie Ihr Kind in die Gestaltung seines Zimmers einbeziehen. Egal ob Ihr Kind eine klare Vorstellung davon hat, wie sein Zimmer aussehen soll, oder nicht – hören Sie ihm zu und versuchen Sie, seine Wünsche zu verstehen. Beteiligen Sie Ihr Kind an der Auswahl funktioneller und ästhetischer Details, wie beispielsweise der Position des Bettes oder der Wandfarbe. Kinder reagieren in unterschiedlichen Altersstufen auch unterschiedlich auf ihre Umgebung.
Denken Sie bei der Gestaltung des Zimmers und der Auswahl der Möbel daran, dass die Entwicklung der Persönlichkeit des Kindes genauso schnell vorangeht wie sein körperliches Wachstum. Sie können sich für den Kauf neuer Möbel entscheiden, wenn Ihr Kind für die alte Einrichtung zu groß geworden ist, oder anpassungsfähige Möbelstücke wählen, die meist teurer sind, sich auf lange Sicht jedoch als weitaus nützlicher und rentabler erweisen.

Kinderkamers zijn de ruimtes waar de kinderen de meeste tijd doorbrengen om te slapen, spelen of studeren. Het centrale element van de slaapkamer is uiteraard het bed, maar een tweede element zal langzaamaan belangrijker worden naarmate het kind ouder wordt: het bureau of de werktafel. En ga niet voorbij aan het belang van een vrije ruimte waar gespeeld kan worden. Uw kind zal er blij mee zijn. Als de kinderkamer groot genoeg is, is het gemakkelijker om hem in verschillende zones te verdelen. Is dit niet het geval dan zult u een beroep moeten doen op inklapbare meubels of op de combinatie van verschillende functies. Er moet speciale aandacht besteed worden aan het creëren van een omgeving die bij de persoonlijkheid van het kind past, zijn nieuwsgierigheid prikkelt en bijdraagt aan zijn persoonlijke ontwikkeling. Het is belangrijk dat het kind deelneemt aan de decoratie van zijn eigen kamer. Kinderen kunnen al dan niet een duidelijk idee hebben over wat ze willen, maar het is voor hen noodzakelijk dat u zich inspant om naar hen te luisteren en hen probeert te begrijpen. Betrek de kinderen bij functionele en esthetische details zoals de manier waarop het bed wordt neergezet of de kleur waarin de wanden worden geverfd. Naargelang hun leeftijd, staan kinderen op een andere manier in verband met hun omgeving.
U weet hoe snel kinderen groeien en dus ook hun persoonlijkheid. Houd daar rekening mee wanneer u de kamer ontwerpt en de meubels uitkiest. Het is mogelijk om nieuwe meubels te kopen naarmate uw kind ouder wordt of om aanpasbaar meubilair te zoeken, dat gewoonlijk duurder maar op lange termijn absoluut nuttiger en rendabeler is.

La camera è il luogo in cui i bambini trascorrono più tempo dormendo, giocando o studiando. L'elemento centrale della camera è, ovviamente, il letto, anche se un secondo elemento acquisisce sempre più importanza via via che il bambino cresce: la scrivania o il tavolo da lavoro. Non è poi da trascurare lo spazio libero che servirà come zona gioco, particolarmente apprezzato dal bambino. Se la camera è abbastanza grande, sarà più facile suddividerla in zone. In caso contrario sarà necessario ricorrere a mobili richiudibili o in grado di svolgere molteplici funzioni. Sarà necessario creare un ambiente affine alla personalità del bambino, che stimoli la sua curiosità e contribuisca al suo sviluppo personale. È importante che il piccolo partecipi alla decorazione della propria stanza. Anche se i bambini possono non avere un'idea chiara di ciò che desiderano, conviene fare uno sforzo e cercare di ascoltarli e comprenderne desideri e necessità. Può essere utile coinvolgerli nella scelta dei dettagli funzionali ed estetici come l'ubicazione del letto o il colore delle pareti. I bambini si rapportano all'ambiente che li circonda in modo diverso in base all'età. Tutti sanno con quale velocità i bambini crescano e sviluppino la propria personalità. Questo aspetto andrà considerato al momento di progettare la sua cameretta e scegliere gli arredi. Si potrà poi scegliere se rinnovare gli arredi via via che il bambino cresce oppure acquistare mobili adattabili, solitamente più cari ma senza dubbio più utili ed economici sul lungo termine.

El dormitorio es la estancia donde los niños pasan más tiempo, ya sea durmiendo, jugando o estudiando. El elemento central del dormitorio, por supuesto, es la cama, si bien un segundo elemento cobrará protagonismo conforme el pequeño vaya creciendo: el escritorio o la mesa de trabajo. No debemos pasar por alto el espacio despejado que servirá como zona de juegos. Nuestros hijos lo agradecerán. Si el dormitorio es lo bastante amplio, resultará más fácil dividirlo en zonas. En caso contrario, tendremos que recurrir a mobiliario plegable o combinar distintas funciones. Debemos poner especial atención en la creación de un entorno afín a la personalidad del niño, que estimule su curiosidad y contribuya a su desarrollo personal. Es importante que el pequeño participe en la decoración de su propia habitación. Los niños pueden o no tener una idea clara de lo que quieren, pero conviene hacer el esfuerzo de escucharlos y entenderlos, y hacerlos participar en la elección de los detalles funcionales y estéticos, como la ubicación de la cama o el color de las paredes. Los niños se relacionan de modos distintos con su entorno en función de su edad.
Es bien sabida la rapidez con la que crecen los niños y con la que desarrollan sus personalidades. Debemos tenerlo en cuenta a la hora de diseñar su dormitorio y escoger el mobiliario. Podemos optar entre renovar el mobiliario cuando crezcan o buscar muebles adaptables, por lo común más caros pero sin duda más útiles y rentables a largo plazo.

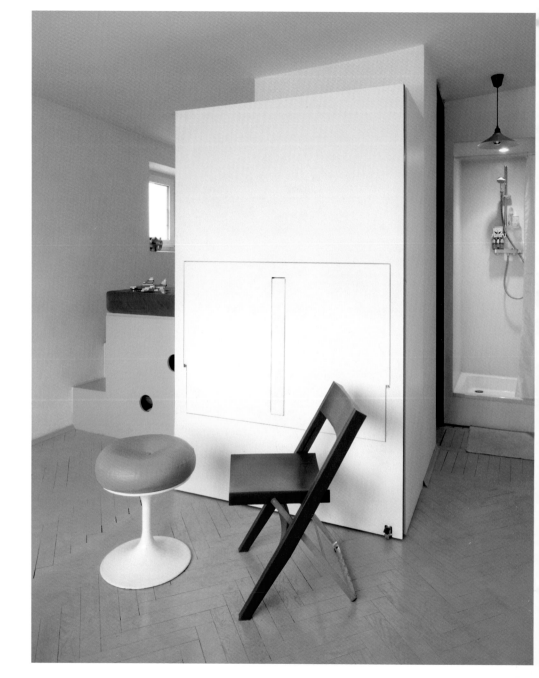

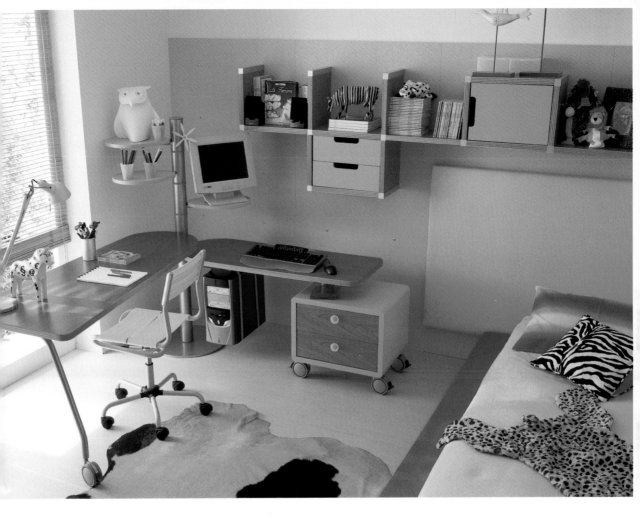

403

413

415

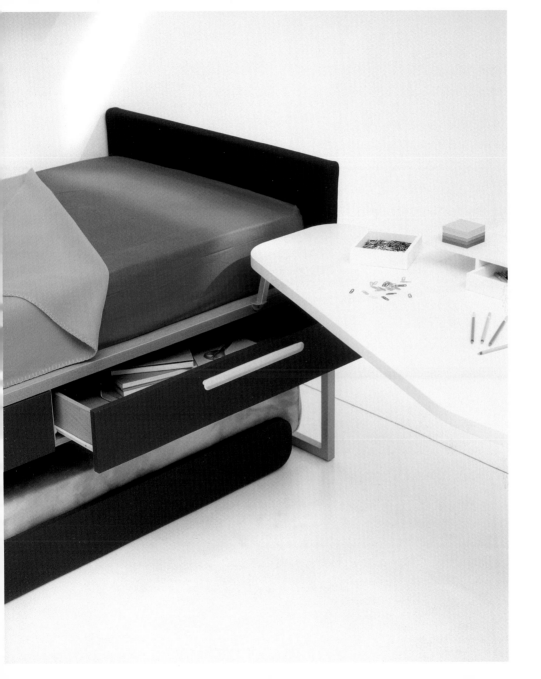

BATHROOMS

SALLES DE BAINS

BADEZIMMER

BADKAMERS

BAGNO

CUARTOS DE BAÑO

Bathrooms are usually cluttered up with plumbing fixtures, cabinets, mirrors and other installations, bringing a higher level of complexity to the space. There also tends to be a wider range of finish materials in the bathrooms: stone or tile countertops, white enamel fixtures and chrome fittings, glass partitions and mirrors, ceramic tile walls and floors and the accessories. When dealing with a small bathroom, it is a good idea to start assembling your material selection with the least flexible ones: perhaps the fixtures and the wall and floor finishes.

When it comes to surface finishes, there are two prevalent styles in contemporary bathroom design: mosaics and natural stone. Mosaic tiles allow to introduce color and create contrast with the stark white fixtures for example. You can delimit areas such as the shower or create patterns. Natural stone such as slate, limestone and, of course, marble are suitable materials to dress up your bathroom. Slate confers the bathroom with a stylish character but needs to be used sparingly if the bathroom is small. Limestone adds a natural look. Limestone is available in polished and honed finish. Take this into account when selecting the tiles to either give your bathroom a sharp and sophisticated look or a natural and rustic quality.

If you decide to go for a more creative approach and minimize the use of tile, consider using richly patterned wall paper or deep paint colors. And remember that the final touches are brought in by the small details such as the towels, bathmat, mirrors and other accessories.

Les salles de bains sont généralement encombrées de pièces de robinetterie, de placards, de miroirs et d'autres éléments qui rendent ces espaces plus complexes. En général, les salles de bains présentent également une grande variété de finitions : comptoirs en carreau ou en pierre, robinetterie en émail blanc, accessoires chromés, cloisons en verre, miroirs, murs et sols en céramique, accessoires. Lorsqu'il s'agit d'une petite salle de bains, il est judicieux de commencer par le choix de matériaux qui soient en accord avec les éléments les moins flexibles : la robinetterie, les finitions des murs et des sols.

Pour ce qui concerne les revêtements, deux styles prévalent dans le design contemporain des salles de bains : les mosaïques et la pierre naturelle. Les carreaux de mosaïque permettent d'introduire de la couleur et de créer un contraste avec le blanc de la robinetterie par exemple. Vous pouvez délimiter certaines zones, comme la douche, ou bien créer des motifs. Les pierres naturelles telles que l'ardoise, la pierre à chaux et, bien sûr, le marbre sont des matériaux parfaits pour habiller une salle de bains. L'ardoise confère une touche élégante mais il faut l'utiliser avec parcimonie si la pièce est petite. La pierre à chaux ajoute un côté naturel. Vous pouvez la trouver polie ou aiguisée. Prenez cela en considération au moment de choisir les carreaux de votre salle de bains, afin de lui conférer un aspect soigné et sophistiqué, ou bien naturel et rustique.

Si vous décidez de choisir une approche plus créative et de minimiser l'utilisation de carreaux, envisagez un papier peint riche en motifs ou des peintures de couleurs vives. Souvenez-vous aussi que les touches finales sont apportées par les petits détails tels que les serviettes, les tapis de bains, les miroirs et autres accessoires.

Da ein Badezimmer üblicherweise voll ist mit Armaturen, Schränken, Spiegeln und anderen Elementen, muss der vorhandene Platz klug ausgenutzt werden. Für diesen Raum stehen meist zahlreiche Materialien und Oberflächenbearbeitungen zur Auswahl: Waschtische mit einer Oberfläche aus Stein oder Fliesen, Armaturen aus weißem Emaille und Chrom, Glastrennwände, Spiegel, Wandverkleidungen und Bodenbeläge aus Keramikfliesen sowie unzählige Badezimmeraccessoires. Bei kleinen Bädern sollte man bei der Materialauswahl mit den Elementen beginnen, die am wenigsten flexibel sind, wie z. B. mit den Armaturen, der Wandverkleidung und dem Bodenbelag.

Was die Oberflächen anbelangt, so sind im Bereich der zeitgenössischen Badezimmergestaltung derzeit vor allem zwei Stilrichtungen angesagt: Mosaikfliesen und Naturstein. Mosaikfliesen bringen Farbe ins Bad und schaffen einen lebendigen Kontrast zur schlichten weißen Sanitärkeramik. Außerdem können sie zur optischen Abtrennung einzelner Bereiche, wie z. B. der Dusche, und zur Gestaltung von Mustern eingesetzt werden. Natursteinfliesen wie beispielsweise aus Schiefer, Kalkstein und natürlich Marmor sind bestens geeignet, um ein Bad hochwertig auszustatten. Schiefer verleiht dem Badezimmer eine erlesene Note, sollte in kleinen Bädern jedoch keinesfalls großflächig eingesetzt werden. Kalksteinfliesen sorgen für einen natürlichen Touch und sind poliert oder geschliffen erhältlich. Berücksichtigen Sie dies bei der Auswahl der Fliesen, um Ihrem Badezimmer je nach Wunsch einen schicken, raffinierten Look oder eine natürliche, rustikale Note zu verleihen.

Wenn Sie eine kreativere Gestaltung bevorzugen und die Verwendung von Fliesen auf ein Minimum beschränken möchten, sollten Sie eine groß gemusterte Tapete oder kräftige Wandfarben in Erwägung ziehen. Den letzten Schliff verleihen Sie Ihrem Badezimmer mit Accessoires wie Handtüchern, Badvorleger, Spiegel usw.

Badkamers zijn meestal volgepropt met sanitair, kasten, spiegels en andere spullen waardoor zij complexer zijn om in te richten. Daarentegen is het assortiment beschikbare materialen voor badkamers ook groter: marmer of tegels voor werkbladen, witgelakte en verchroomde accessoires, glasschermen en spiegels, tegelwanden en -vloeren en diverse andere details. Wanneer men een kleine badkamer heeft, is het een goed idee om eerst het materiaal te selecteren, beginnend bij de minst flexibele materialen: wellicht sanitair en de wand- en vloerafwerkingen.

Wat betreft de afwerkingen van oppervlakken hebben twee stijlen de overhand in het moderne design van badkamers: mozaïeken en natuursteen. Mozaïektegeltjes zorgen voor kleur en creëren een contrast met het strakke wit van bijvoorbeeld het sanitair. Ze kunnen worden gebruikt om zones zoals de douche af te bakenen of om dessins te creëren. Natuursteen, zoals leisteen, kalksteen en natuurlijk marmer, is ideaal materiaal voor de decoratie van uw badkamer. Leisteen geeft de badkamer stijl, hoewel het wel met mate moet worden toegepast als de badkamer erg klein is. Kalksteen zorgt voor een natuurlijke uitstraling. Het is verkrijgbaar in een gepolijste of grove afwerking. Houd hiermee rekening wanneer u de tegels uitzoekt en ervoor kiest om uw badkamer met een elegante en geraffineerde stijl in te richten of hem liever een natuurlijke en rustieke uitstraling te geven.

Als u voor een creativere aanpak kiest en het gebruik van tegels wilt minimaliseren, overweeg dan de mogelijkheid om bedrukt behang of verf in felle kleuren te gebruiken. En vergeet niet dat kleine details zoals handdoeken, badmatten, spiegels en andere accessoires voor de finishing touch zorgen.

Le stanze da bagno sono costituite da un insieme di tubi, pensili, specchi e altri elementi tecnici che danno vita a uno spazio più complesso di altri. D'altra parte, anche la gamma di materiali per le finiture è più diversificata: marmo o mattonelle per i ripiani, accessori laccati di bianco e altri cromati, divisori in vetro e specchi, pareti e pavimenti a mattonelle, oltre a vari altri complementi. Quando si deve organizzare un bagno di piccole dimensioni, conviene iniziare dalla scelta dei materiali partendo da quelli che offrono una minore flessibilità come il wc, la doccia o la vasca, il bidet e il lavabo e poi le finiture delle pareti e del pavimento. Per quanto riguarda le superfici, nella progettazione dei bagni contemporanei prevalgono due stili: i mosaici e la pietra naturale. Le tessere di mosaico apportano colore e creano un contrasto con il bianco puro degli elementi del bagno e possono essere utilizzate per delimitare zone come la doccia o per creare disegni. La pietra naturale come la lavagna, la pietra calcarea e - ovviamente- il marmo è un materiale particolarmente adatto per il bagno. La lavagna trasmette stile al bagno, anche se va usata con moderazione nel caso di ambienti piccoli. La pietra calcarea apporta un tocco naturale ed è disponibile nella finitura liscia o grezza. Questo elemento andrà considerato al momento di scegliere le mattonelle e decidere se conferire al bagno un aspetto elegante e sofisticato o piuttosto naturale e rustico.
Qualora si decida di scommettere su un approccio più creativo e ridurre al minimo l'uso di mattonelle, una buona soluzione può essere quella di scegliere la carta da parati stampata o una vernice dai colori vivaci. È importante ricordare che il tocco finale viene dato dai piccoli dettagli come gli asciugamani, il tappeto della doccia, gli specchi e altri accessori.

Los cuartos de baño suelen ser un compendio de tuberías, armarios, espejos y otras instalaciones, todo lo cual genera un espacio con un mayor grado de complejidad. Por otra parte, la gama de materiales de acabados también suele ser más amplia: mármol o baldosas para las encimeras, accesorios lacados en blanco y otros cromados, mamparas de vidrio y espejos, paredes y suelos embaldosados y complementos varios. A la hora de abordar un cuarto de baño pequeño conviene empezar por organizar la selección de materiales a partir de los menos flexibles, probablemente los del inodoro, la ducha o bañera, el bidé y el lavabo, y los acabados de paredes y suelo.
En lo tocante a los acabados de superficies, en el diseño de baños contemporáneo prevalecen dos estilos: los mosaicos y la piedra natural. Las teselas de mosaico aportan color y crean contraste con el crudo blanco de los elementos del cuarto de baño, por ejemplo. Pueden usarse para delimitar zonas como la ducha o para crear dibujos. La piedra natural, como la pizarra, la caliza y, por supuesto, el mármol, son materiales idóneos para decorar el baño. La pizarra aporta al cuarto de baño estilo, si bien debe usarse con moderación si la estancia es pequeña. La piedra caliza aporta un toque natural. Está disponible en acabado pulido o tosco. Debemos tenerlo en cuenta a la hora de seleccionar las baldosas y decidir si preferimos imprimir al cuarto de baño un aspecto elegante y sofisticado o más bien natural y rústico.
Si decidimos apostar por un enfoque más creativo y minimizar el uso de las baldosas, hemos de sopesar la posibilidad de utilizar papel pintado estampado o pintura de colores vivos. Y no olvidemos que los toques finales los aportan pequeños detalles como las toallas, la alfombra de la ducha, los espejos y otros accesorios.

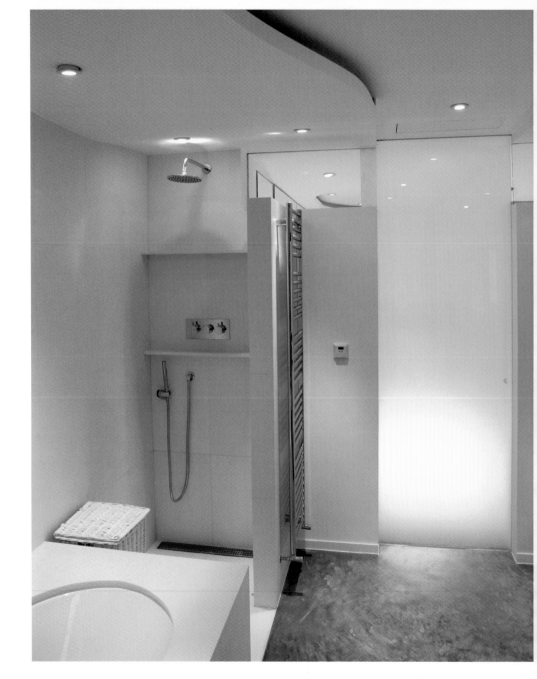

Raumteam
Weißkirchen, Austria
www.raumteam.at
© Stefan Meyer: p. 42-43, 44, 45

Ruiz-Velazquez Architecture and Design
Madrid, Spain
www.ruizvelazquez.com
© Pedro Martínez: p. 116 left, 212, 213 top, 242, 484

S.DREI Architektur
Graz, Austria
www.sdrei.com
© Angelo Kaunat: p. 108, 173, 177, 253, 265
© Bernd Steinhuber: p. 258, 259

Satoshi Kurosaki/APOLLO Architects & Associates
Tokyo, Japan; Seoul, South Korea
www.kurosakisatoshi.com
© Masao Nishikawa: p. 296 left

Schmidt
Worldwide
www.schmidt-cocinas.es
© Schmidt: p. 283

Silvestri Architettura
Genoa, Italy
www.silvestri.info
© Roberto Silvestri: p. 436, 437

Simone Micheli Architectural Hero
Florence and Milan, Italy
www.simonemicheli.com
© Jürgen Eheim: p. 266, 413, 438

Six Degrees Architects
Melbourne, Australia
www.sixdegrees.com.au
© Shania Shegedyn: p. 24-25

SPaN – Stonely Pelsinski architects Neukomm
New York, NY, USA
www.span-ny.com
© Michael Moran: p. 92, 93, 144, 145, 206, 207, 287

Splitterwerk
Graz, Austria
http://splitterwerk.at
© Paul Ott: p. 40, 41

Studio Guilherme Torres
São Paulo, Brazil
www.guilhermetorres.com
© MCA Estúdio: p. 69 right, 160, 161, 198, 199, 267, 320

Studio Uribe
Miami Beach, FL, USA; London, United Kingdom
www.studiouribe.com
© Claudia Uribe: p. 48, 134

Tad & Jessica Carpenter
Kansas City, MO, USA
http://tadcarpenter.com
© Eric Linebarger/LemonLime Photography: p. 62, 87, 106, 107, 216, 248, 249, 342-343

Tervhivatal
Budapest, Hungary
http://www.tervhivatal.hu/
© Tamás Bujnovszky: p. 458, 459

Tisettanta
Milan and Turin, Italy; London, United Kingdom
www.tisettanta.com
© Tisettanta: p. 405

VSAconcept*
Antwerp, Belgium
http://www.wix.com/vsaconcept/vsaconcept/contact#!
© Vehap Shehi: p. 130, 270, 271, 330, 331

Vora Arquitectura
Barcelona, Spain; Lisbon, Portugal
www.vora-arquitectura.com
© Adrià Goula: p. 256, 257

Yoshihara McKee Architect
New York, NY, USA
www.yoshiharamckee.com
© Julian Wass: p. 109, 175
© Hiroki Yoshihara: p. 174, 250, 251, 346, 347, 486, 487